THE BODIES THAT REMAIN

Before you start to read this book, take this moment to think about making a donation to punctum books, an independent non-profit press,

@ https://punctumbooks.com/support/

If you're reading the e-book, you can click on the image below to go directly to our donations site. Any amount, no matter the size, is appreciated and will help us to keep our ship of fools afloat. Contributions from dedicated readers will also help us to keep our commons open and to cultivate new work that can't find a welcoming port elsewhere. Our adventure is not possible without your support.

Vive la open-access.

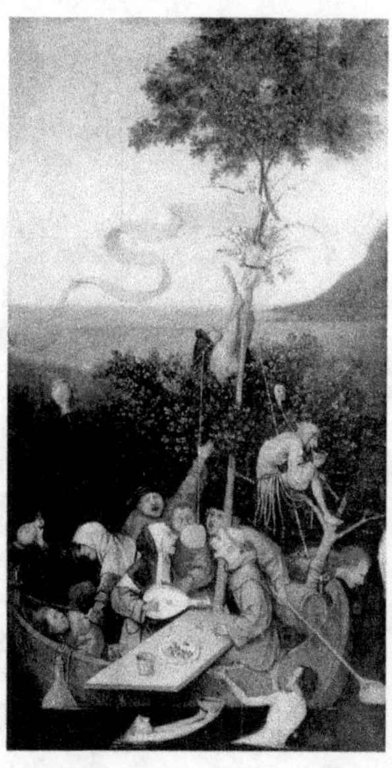

Fig. 1. Hieronymus Bosch, *Ship of Fools* (1490–1500)

First published in 2018 by dead letter office, BABEL Working Group
an imprint of punctum books, Earth, Milky Way.
https://punctumbooks.com

The BABEL Working Group is a collective and desiring-assemblage of scholar–gypsies with no leaders or followers, no top and no bottom, and only a middle. BABEL roams and stalks the ruins of the post-historical university as a multiplicity, a pack, looking for other roaming packs with which to cohabit and build temporary shelters for intellectual vagabonds. We also take in strays.

ISBN-13: 978-1-947447-67-7 (print)
ISBN-13: 978-1-947447-68-4 (ePDF)

LCCN: 2018946359
Library of Congress Cataloging Data is available from the Library of Congress

Book design: Vincent W.J. van Gerven Oei
Cover image: Alex Simpson, *within, without,* 2015.
Frontispiece: Mike Harvey

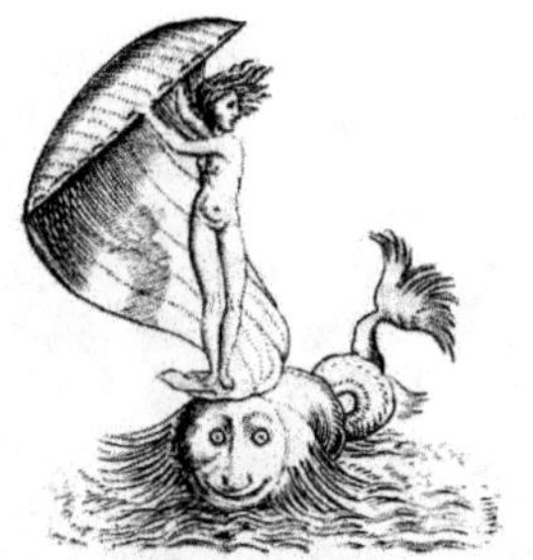

HIC SVNT MONSTRA

THE BODIES THAT REMAIN

Edited by Emmy Beber

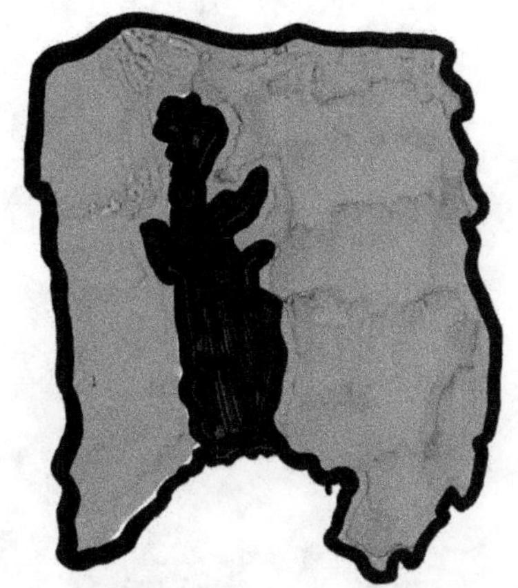

~~Between the poles of Trickster and Boogy~~
~~Sensible scribbles and Devil's advocates~~
~~haggle over a pile of the writhing guts~~

this was yer knee

For family

Contents

Introduction

Emmy Beber

"To love, bodily."
Gillian Rose

✡

The Bodies That Remain arrived on its own terms. I spent the next two years gathering examples. Throughout the process people would ask me periodically if I understood the book as a 'body of work'. It was a collection, so this was a possibility. But somehow this felt too complete. The only physical body I had ever known truly was chaotic, anxious, constantly moving. At the beginning, the book felt like this too; it was unpredictable. The writing within shifted form, changed tone, pace, even subject; as though scattered parts, the texts arrived in my inbox from studios in New York, Philadelphia, Chicago; from hillsides in Yorkshire and the silent landscapes of the French countryside; from London back rooms, Belfast laboratories and even from aboard ship, in the middle of the ocean. It was a peculiar experience coming to care *viscerally* about the words of others as though it were their bodies I was working with; caring for the bodies being spoken about — the fictions, truths, pain, the sharing of bodies and their absences; learning how to allow a body to appear in writing without becoming the body.

The Bodies That Remain could never become a 'body of work' complete because those bodies being written about had written themselves into the future, had shaped the bodies of their readers, their writers and would move beyond. The boundary was too tight. These were bodies whose boundaries remained malleable and even in their absences had refused to expire.

Where 'body' as a verb makes material something abstract, *The Bodies That Remain,* as a collection, became bodily.

✲

How do you reproduce the resistance between the body and its attempt to articulate? To allow the writing to remain uncomfortable performing the inarticulacy of the body — its falters, stutters, spillages – is to attend to the body through language, is to attend to movement; the page changes texture, the words unable to remain still. Or, broken, they lie flat on the page, unmoving.

"If you want to exist, you must accept flesh and the moment." Jeff Nuttall wrote through the body and his was the first work I grappled with its attention to all things physical. Our language of the body was different but translated it had a shared urgency. When you write the body, you remain within and perform it. Language becomes movement, becomes moment. The urgency I was looking for was interstitial. It was the space between the body physical and the body as it performed itself. How could I turn this into something familiar? Nuttall had devoured all of the body writers before him and I would do the same. I could list the names of some of the writers I worked my way through: Michel Leiris, Roland Bathes, Nathalie Sarraute; Eileen Myles, Hilton Als, Kathy Acker; Susan Sontag, Maggie Nelson, Wayne Koestenbaum; Lynne Tillman, Ben Marcus, Marguerite Duras, and on and on and on.

Each writer could be traced back, each had an entire lineage of other body writers worked through. Though not all directly confronted or involved the body as object within their work, there were residues; language stuttered, remained surprising, moving.

In London I began working with children and realised very quickly that we are taught how to use our bodies. I had to retrain myself to write in a way far removed from my own syncopated scrawl. Their writing understands the body as a thing made by them, able to change its properties. Their surfaces are malleable and those tools that allow them to share their ideas have to be invited in. I thought about Robert Walser's ever shrinking pencil as I watched a child press pencil into page, how Walser's writing became smaller and smaller. The children notice everything about their body and yours and are happy to tell you. As a child, my writing was microscopic and remains so to this day. Theirs sits boldly on the line, biting back at the pencil that made them. As a child, before being taught, your body remains out of time.

In a moment of pause, I read Gillian Rose's *Love's Work*, Margueritte Duras's *La douer* and Emily LaBarge's PhD chapters *The Essay as Form* and thought about the sounds of the body in horror, in mourning, in truth. The body trying to escape itself; Rose describing her want to create an ethnography of shit in the face of seeing her body outside of body, the colostomy bag; the truths or weight of the body as form. The function of the sounds is to make us stop being a body altogether. Yet the body becomes this. Becomes language, becomes writing. As Gillian Rose said, "to love, bodily". Emotions remains mortal, must remain mortal *or else they are nothing.*

✵

The most I have learnt about language and the body has been from the writers in this book. It was Philip Hoare telling me about his experience of discovering ambergris in a nook of the ocean and his transferring a small smudge of it from sea to his hand, from his hand to the notebook and the stench that remained. It was talking with Tai Shani about how delicious a description of flesh might be, how we are shaped by the bodies of others, by the space around them and their movement. It was Lynne Tillman writing Jane Bowles' disappearance and reappearance, her restlessness in life and successful dispersal at burial, a line drawing of movement across language. It was Mike Harvey's endless fascination with the meshing and reforming of the body through scabbing and the fierce conversations with Claire Potter on body trauma, how language can show the impoverishment of itself as a performance of bodily experiences made inarticulate. It was reading Mairead Case writing, "When I read and write I know I'm moving somehow. I know my body's holding space." The back and forth emails of chlorine soaked lido skin with Heather Phillipson and the stories from Chloé Griffin on the impossibility of the body of water she was sailing over that week, of her new geographies, their sounds and scents and colour. Devouring Harman Bains' writings, I learnt much on the erotic body in its many guises and curiosities, and I learnt the body as something other — nourishing my own — from the books and essays and stories from Pil and Galia Kollectiv. The ongoing conversation with Kevin Breathnach taught me about the multitude of expressions and odours the body can erupt, the emails with Emily LaBarge about how language can eventually turn on the body, can expose it, and through the sharing of stories and our own experiences with Phoebe Blatton, I learnt what it is to understand how to be within a body. I have stories for every contributor. It has been a privilege to share mind spaces with all of them. Their words have shaped my understanding of writing the body and being a body.

✲

On a car journey recently I had a conversation with my friend who works in palliative care about death. She told me how those that are restless in life, who can never sit still, are often restless at death, they refuse their end. The bodies within this book remain restless and even in their absence find new ways of being. Molded into the lives of their writers are their bodies, in language. Echoes of the shape of their thinking.

1

The Life and Deaths of Jane Bowles (or, Reputation)

Lynne Tillman

Jane Bowles was born on February 22, 1917, a short, usually harsh month — it seems right for her. Bowles's unique writing and life were cut short, derailed by neuroses, alcoholism, physical illness. Her friends remember her sharp wit, agile mind, gaiety, humor, outrageousness. While she lived, stories about wild Jane Bowles circulated in Tangier where she resided from 1948. Back then she was a living legend, but the flux of reputation — here today, gone tomorrow — sends her body of work into and out of print (OP).

Among certain contemporary writers, including Lydia Davis, Deborah Eisenberg, Michael Cunningham, Jane Bowles is celebrated and revered for her work, notably her sole, singular novel *Two Serious Ladies* (1943).[1] It has also been praised exuberantly by Tennessee Williams, Truman Capote, and John Ashbery. Bowles finished six stories, and a play, *In The Summer House*, which ran on Broadway in 1954, with incidental music by Paul Bowles.

Jane Bowles didn't subscribe to what life held in store for her, an upper-middle-class Jewish-American girl from Woodmere,

1 Jane Bowles, 'Two Serious Ladies', in *The Collected Works of Jane Bowles* (New York: Farrar, Straus, & Giroux, New York, 1966), 3–201.

Long Island, New York. Willfully, it seems, she undid her putative future; the unexpected — accidents of fate — also changed it: the death of her adored father, when she was 13, and, then, as an adolescent, she developed tuberculosis in her knee. The teenager recovered in a Swiss hospital, her leg in traction for months, when, it is said, she discovered her love of reading and literature. Ever after, she walked with a limp. Paul Bowles' hated, anti-Semitic father called her 'that crippled kike'.

Out of her mother's house, according to Millicent Dillon in her definitive biography, *A Little Original Sin,*[2] Bowles rebelled hard and fast. She led a super-fueled young adulthood, hanging out with writers and artists, bar-hopping in Greenwich Village, pursuing love and sex with other women. She was adamant in her desire for thrill, a Bohemian when the term meant something. Composer Paul Bowles and she met in 1937, and, surprising everyone, they married in 1938.

Bowles rejected comfort and complacency; she disdained middle-class values. Ease never befriended her: She questioned everything. 'I had met nervous girls before', Tennessee Williams wrote in his preface to *Feminine Wiles,* 'but her quicksilver animation, her continual cries to me and herself: 'Shall we do this or that? What shall we do?' showed such an extreme kind of excited indecision....'[3]

Reading her work, I can feel that anxiety in slight shifts of tone, in her unusual juxtapositions, both jarring and productive. I read her phrases again and again, adjectives abutting nouns in unlikely relationships, an innovativeness with language that she shared with Jean Rhys. I might become melancholy, reading her, though her writing also makes me laugh out loud, the way Kafka's does. But Kafka's work is cooler. He's observing his writing and himself writing it. His work, in a sense, depends on distance — between psyche and society. He writes about and

2 Millicent Dillon, *A Little Original Sin: The Life and Work of Jane Bowles* (Berkeley: University of California Press, 1998).

3 Tennessee Williams, 'Introduction' to Jane Bowles, *Feminine Wiles* (Santa Barbara: Black Sparrow Press, 1976), 7–8. This is a collection of Bowles' unfinished stories.

with detachment. Bowles is not detached, not in any way; her irony might even have boomeranged on her.

The way she lived differed starkly from her middle-class beginnings, but more the way she wrote veered from conventional literary modernisms. In writing, she didn't pursue a self; I can't imagine she believed one existed. She didn't write to discover an identity. She denied identifications and worked toward disidentifications. While a sense of the fragmented underlay her order of things, she didn't strive for it. Her metier was seams and fissures.

A Jane Bowles character, like its author, will have trouble making up her or his mind. I take 'making up one's mind' literally: minds are made, not born. Bowles was exceedingly conscious of this and stymied by it. She was kept in doubt, undone by right and wrong, by what she didn't know, and what could be in her mind without her wanting it. Bowles' characters play in this absurdity, having choice and no choice simultaneously. Irrationality ineluctably figures into action and inaction, causing contradictions, and sometimes paralysis.

Any sentence from *Two Serious Ladies* displays Jane Bowles' disorienting, elegant style — in fact, any sentence from all of her writing:

> Arnold had just taken quite a large bite of his sandwich so that he was unable to answer her [Miss Gamelon]. But he did roll his eyes in her direction. It was impossible to tell with his cheeks so full whether or not he was angry. Miss Gamelon was terribly annoyed at this, but Miss Goering sat smiling at them because she was glad to have them both with her again.[4]

The movement from Arnold's cheeks, to Miss Gamelon's reaction to him, to Miss Goering's feelings about them, makes a sketch of each — I want to say, they're line drawings. Arnold's full cheeks can't be read as angry or not, which annoys Miss Gamelon, while

4 Bowles, 'Two Serious Ladies', 117.

Miss Goering smiles, happy to be with them. A reader can see the composition at the table, these three curious beings.

(I wonder: What troubled Jane Bowles when she wrote those sentences, which words worried her, what made her anxious.)

All choice — in life, writing — pained her. Making a choice, which writing allows and supposedly encourages — be as free as you can be! — created perpetual havoc. Working on the exceptional short story, 'Camp Cataract', Jane got stuck. She told Paul Bowles that she couldn't name a kind of bridge, cantilevered, unless she knew exactly how it was built. She made no assumptions even about her mother tongue, and said No to the first thing that came to mind. Her mind saw fit to unmake even plain words and phrases, to unveil home truths' hidden messages. Writing turned into a representation of her intensity and fierce integrity, she wanted honesty in language and syntax.

Like everyone else, Jane Bowles's volition was regularly compromised, and she moved to dictates she couldn't know. Psychoanalytically, home is always where you go, and, though Jane Bowles left hers to be herself, let's say, or to figure out her own way of life, or to write, she appears to have been unsatisfied, always restless. She and Paul Bowles, dedicated to difference, to being strangers in a strange land, chose their new home, but no place was home, I think, for her, and she didn't find it in her writing, either.

Paul Bowles found an odd comfort in estrangement; it suited his disposition, his dry humor. His story 'You Are Not I' is a tale of psychological horror, of a young girl's 'madness', and sent proverbial chills down this reader's spine. Jane Bowles' stories weren't horrifying or cold-blooded. Nothing she wrote is like Paul's 'Pages from Cold Point', a father/son incest story in which the son is the predator. The kind of horror she understood seeped into ordinary events and daily obligations that had to be faced, couldn't ever be avoided, and where deception lay in wait.

Jane Bowles portrayed all societies as unforgiving and alienating. Her writing oxymoronically sustains a condition of permanent disorientation.

The short story 'Everything Is Nice' begins:

> The highest street in the Blue Moslem town skirted the edge of a cliff. She walked over to the thick protecting wall and looked down. The tide was out, and the flat dirty rocks below were swarming with skinny boys. A Moslem woman came up to the blue wall and stood next to her, grazing her hip with the basket she was carrying.[5]

In this 'blue Moslem town', everything is nice and strange, for Jeanie. The Muslim woman, Zodelia, calls her a Nazarene.

> 'Where is your mother?' Zodelia said at length.'
>
> 'My mother is in the country in her own house,' she said automatically; she had answered the question a hundred times.
>
> 'Why don't you write her a letter and tell her to come here?'[6]

To Zodelia, Jeanie's mother living so far away is weird, maybe unthinkable, certainly not nice. Later, Zodelia pointedly inquires about Jeanie's aunt: 'Where *is* she?' (The italic 'is' is Bowles'.)

Her fictional characters often track homeward. Bowles's own sense of exclusion, of being on the outside, was powerful. She wanted to belong, somewhere, and 'home' is a problem and question in most of her work.

But home or away, life was very strange, and it was also frightening. That is ever-present in Bowles' writing. She seems to say, 'This is how it goes.' Life is incomprehensible, existence is bizarre, unaccountable, mean. There may be beauty or joy, momentary as a parting glance, so her characters will hope for even momentary happiness, as does Jeanie — genie — when she rushes out into the unknown to feel it before it goes.

Two Serious Ladies's protagonists, Miss Goering and Mrs. Copperfield, leave home, bearing opposite psychologies: Ms.

5 Jane Bowles, 'Everything Is Nice', in *The Collected Works of Jane Bowles*, 313, 315, 319.

6 Ibid., 318.

Goering strikes out, wanting bold adventures, while Mrs. Copperfield trails after her husband, an unwilling traveler/tourist, full of fear. At the end of this seminal, tragi-comic, picaresque novel, they both return home, something their author never did.

Jane Bowles died, in a Spanish hospital, Clinica de Reposa de Los Angeles, run by Catholic nuns, not knowing her name. She lived there — existed — for over five years. The year she died, 1973, the copyright for *Two Serious Ladies* should have been renewed: The law then was to renew copyright 28 years after the date of first copyright. But it wasn't. Jane Bowles died, and the same year her only novel, forgotten by its publisher, was sent into Public Domain.

Tennessee Williams proclaimed, 'I consider her the most important writer of prose fiction in modern American letters.'[7] This most important writer's body of work summarily disappeared, and, ironically, sadly, absurdly, her corpse did, too. Upon her death, Paul Bowles had her body interred in a cemetery in San Miguel, Malaga, but leased the plot for only ten years, then let it lapse. The location of her grave became a mystery, and, without a renewed lease, '[b]ecause no one had claimed Jane's remains in response to official notification, her body would [have been] thrown into a common grave.'[8] Let's say, the public domain for corpses.

Paul Bowles built his own shrine to Jane Bowles in his apartment in Tangier. He dedicated a wooden shelf to her books in all their editions and translations. (I visited his home in 1987.) Ultimately, though he had no truck with graves or an after-life, he permitted a young student, enamored of Jane Bowles, to move her body to another cemetery (the cemetery where JB had been buried might itself be buried under a highway).[9] The young woman was rebuffed by Malaga officials, who suddenly decided Jane Bowles' grave was important to the city's cultural history.

7 Williams, 'Introduction', 7.

8 Millicent Dillon, 'Keeper of the Flame', *The New Yorker*, 27 January 1997, https://www.newyorker.com/magazine/1997/01/27/keeper-of-the-flame-2.

9 Ibid.

Bowles' skull and bones have had a very peculiar trajectory, if I can call it that, and to say her corpse has been homeless is too cute. It's a long, complicated saga about which both Millicent Dillon and Jon Carlson have given full accounts.[10] To cut to the quick, Bowles's final resting place has depended upon what Tennessee Williams called 'the kindness of strangers.'

Searching for her grave, Jon Carlson found a kindly priest, maybe saintly, called Padre Jose. He had become the keeper of Jane Bowles' flame.

> Padre José said that Jane's new grave, established through the efforts of the municipality of Málaga and the Association of Friends of San Miguel Cemetery, had been unveiled mid-October, 1999. Afterwards, he added secretively, 'But in the evening she moves all over the cemetery, and I am here to watch over her.'[11]

Mentioning her work in conversations; assigning her novel and stories to students, and writing about her, those who treasure Jane Bowles' body of work try to watch over it. Though I'm not completely pessimistic, I regularly observe the literary drift, the burials and un-earthings of writers' reputations. They come and go, 'talking of Michaelangelo,' T.S. Eliot put it, and Eliot also, like Chaucer for 200 years after his death, will likely come and go. Here today, gone tomorrow.

Any writer who believes in her or his literary immortality is delusional. Writers, especially females — Clarice Lispector, for example, who is enjoying a rebirth of interest — writers whose work is mordant, elegant, even grim, their books will disappear. And maybe they'll return from the OP cemetery, rise from the dead, but only if a living person or two feels a great debt to that great writer. And, if that writer's books are reissued, smartly

10 Jon Carlson, 'The Gathering Spirit of Jane Bowles,' *Rain Taxi*, 26 December 2013, http://www.raintaxi.com/the-gathering-spirit-of-jane-bowles/.

11 Ibid.

repackaged, it will have resulted only from vigilance, devotion, and love.

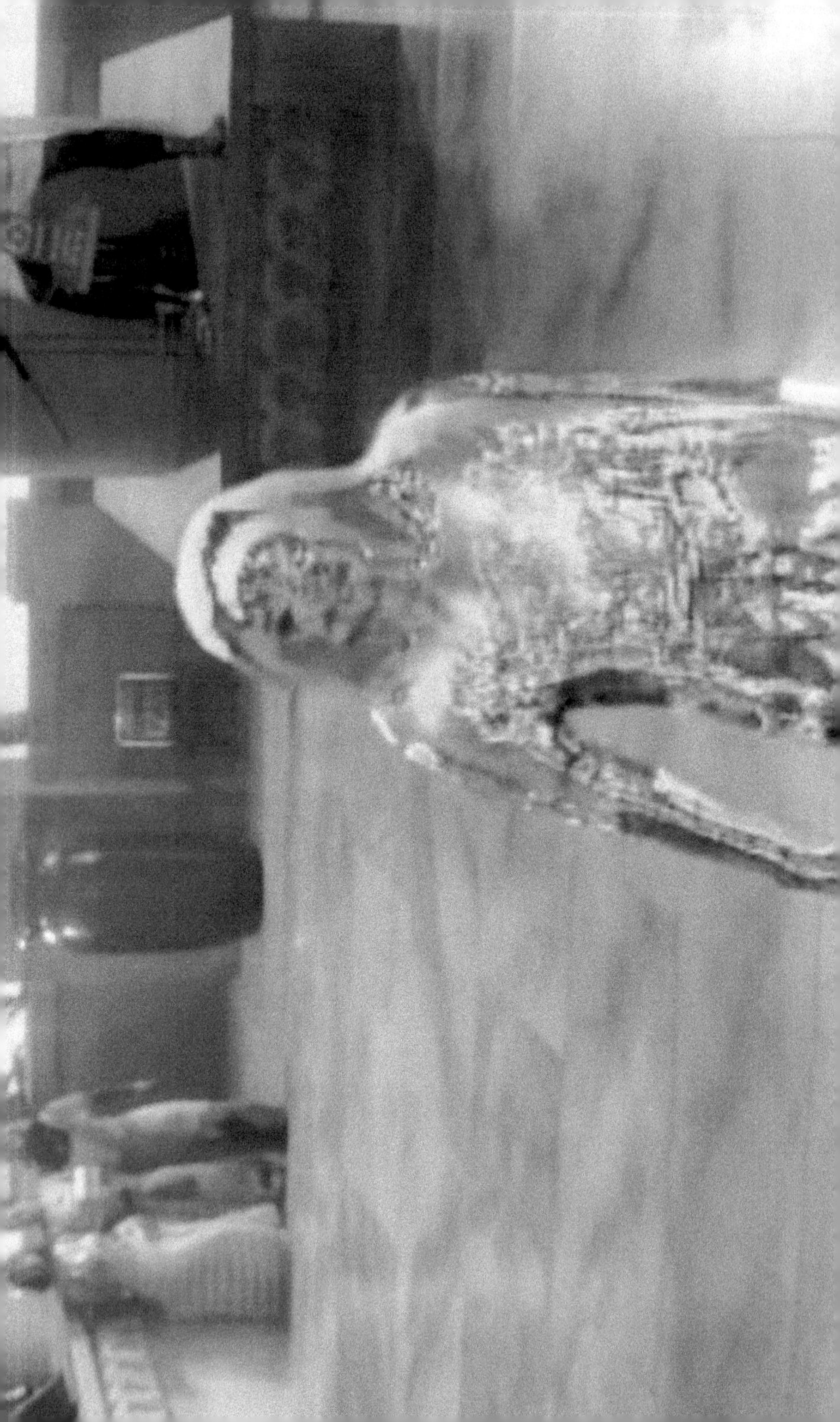

2

Be Michael Jackson

David Rule

Be Michael Jackson. Keep singing, but shrug your shoulders and smile and be lots of different faces and then be Tyra Banks. John Landis yells: 'Cut! That was perfect! How'd you do that???'

Be molten gold. Be the dream of molten gold, all sparkles. Turn into Michael Jackson and seduce the supermodel Iman. Be sand to escape her palace guards.

Be water. Rise up in front of waterfalls and dance. Dance with the shoulders. Turn into Lisa 'Left Eye' Lopes and rap about the problems of the 1990s. Rap 'believe in yourself, the rest is up to me and you.'

Stay water but be a tentacle with a face on it for James Cameron. Learn about tongues. Be the T-1000, be liquid metal again, walk through fire, be disguised as a floor.

Be Odo on Star Trek. Learn to love yourself for who you are, when you could be anything.

Be Michael Jackson in space. Be your sister wearing a sweater in space. Dance together, share the sweater. The sweater is maybe cybergoth and the music video is maybe too expensive.

✵

These faces
so good at singing Michael Jackson
(even Tyra Banks in her own way).
Faces made for mouthwash commercials,
each around for long enough to sing
'It's black! It's white!'
before morphing into other faces
made for shampoo commercials.
Nobody saw Michael Jackson morph
into any of these faces
but it seems possible.
Like when he became molten gold
for the supermodel Iman,
sand to escape her palace guards.
And if that dream of molten gold
(all sparkles) were to survive,
it's not hard to see it in the water
rising up in front of waterfalls
and becoming Lisa 'Left Eye' Lopes
to rap about the problems of the 1990s.
Or in the liquid metal
of the T-1000 becoming a floor.
Or in Odo the changeling alien on Star Trek
who learned to love himself for who he is,
when he could be anything.

In a spaceship Michael Jackson
is turning into his sister.
They dance together, share a sweater,
smash things up.

✵

Tyra Banks sticks out her tongue and turns into different people. And that person smiles and turns into a Calvin Klein-looking model singing 'It's black! It's white!'. Nobody saw Michael Jackson turn into any of these but it seems possible. When director John Landis yells 'Cut! That was perfect! How'd you do that???', Michael Jackson doesn't answer.

Michael Jackson turns into molten gold for the supermodel Iman. It is the dream of molten gold, all sparkles. Totally seduced but wary of comedian Eddie Murphy's jealousy, the supermodel Iman sends her palace guards after Michael Jackson. Michael Jackson turns into sand.

The sand disappears but maybe the water rising up under a waterfall knows something. It turns into Lisa 'Left Eye' Lopes and raps about the problems of the 1990s. The water is not the most real of waters but then we've never seen water dance. With a kind of warning delivered, Lisa 'Left Eye' Lopes turns back into water.

When the water comes back it's science fiction, 'a mimetic polyalloy.' John Conner asks 'What the hell does that mean???' and Arnold Schwarzenegger explains 'Liquid metal.' This liquid metal walks through fire and turns into a floor to hide. In lava it turns inside out.

In space Odo, an alien on Star Trek, learns to love himself for who he is. He can be anything. Each week Odo might be molten gold, dancing water, often a floor.

In a spaceship, Michael Jackson turns into his sister. They dance together, share a sweater. They smash up the most expensive music video. Maybe too expensive. You might want to stop with the excess.

✵

Be molten gold. Be sand. Be your sister wearing a sweater in space. Even water can rise up and dance. Here, shrug your shoulders and smile and be Tyra Banks.

3

Judee Sill

Mairead Case

'Nothing's happened but I think it will soon.'
Judee Sill, 'Crayon Angels'

Bodies are private, performative meatshells. They hold cancers and desire, and pain and joy, and sometimes other bodies too. I realized I had one when I felt sex pleasure, at three, one of my first memories, and also when my mom's shape changed before my little sister was born. I don't know anything about your body unless you tell me. Even if you don't use words, and even though I'll give you water, food, and aspirin anyway, if you have a headache. If some bodies remain, others must not. I feed myself. I believe in ghosts.

Another thing I know is how to hear Judee Sill's voice. Ed gave me two of her albums and right now I listen to them on my way to work. Outside the windows I see mountains, sky, metal-and-wood stands selling fruit and plants. Usually I am drinking lots of coffee very quickly. Crumbling toast in my lap. Judee's voice needed her body to be. Her body isn't here anymore, but its sounds are, somehow, because I can press a button and my ears fill with them. In Judee's absence—in the absence of someone I never met—I feel more myself. I am trying to be as clear as possible here. I don't think any of this is obvious.

I listened to Judee Sill when I lived in Indiana too. I moved there for college, almost fifteen years ago, and I loved her voice because it made me understand my body differently. When I moved to Indiana I was weighted by my body, which I wasn't allowing to menstruate. I thought it must be someone else's because it felt so wrong on me. But when I listened to Judee, I didn't want to put on a binder and makebruises at a show, I wanted to sit in a church and gobble light. I felt released. She sang about crayon angels and enchanted sky machines, lambs, crowns, and cosmos — not white boys like Bikini Kill did. Judee wasn't binary at all.

The very first time I heard her though, was on a mixtape Rob made for a girl he liked. He sent me those tapes too, because they were good and it took him a long time to make them, but also in case of heartbreak. He didn't want to lose the songs. We cared for each other in this awful, tender, childish way. I write about Judee's body by writing about mine. I need my body to hear hers: my ears, the ringing they have sometimes. Some people listen to Judee and never hear ringing. Anyway the song Rob picked was 'Jesus Was a Crossmaker', which is kind of a terrible song to put on a tape for your crush. It's about a stranger, a bandit, and a heartbreaker who sings to his lover then freezes up and smokes off. Judee wrote it for J.D. Souther, a Texan who put her heart through a paper shredder. Rob's logic I guess was that he knew how Judee felt. He'd never be that guy. I want to ask Judee: do we have to fall in love with everyone? And if we do, how do we grow old? Sometimes I would like to be old with lots of lovers. I would like to have this wisdom. That body.

Judee Sill, a beautiful name for a first album by Judee Sill, came out in October 1971 and features Christian mystic lyrics, baroque pop, multiple overdubs, and piano. 'Fuck, man — she's school for all of us', Souther, who wrote songs for the Eagles, told *Rolling Stone*. I found her. I saw her. I tell the magazines.

As a writer I listened first to Judee's lyrics, though later and for the first time I loved how the multiple overdubs of her own voice — mirroring, braiding, climbing — show her growing confidence, or at least her desire to take space. To make it. If Judee could then I could too. I could listen, and stay.

Her lyrics are shimmered, spacy, image-heavy. For example, 'Crayon Angels' features God and a train, the astral plane, magic rings turning fingers green, dead mystic roses, and phony prophets. What hit me here was the idea that images — which need space to be, like bodies do — can communicate, can connect with something — the church, punk shows — even if they don't agree with all of it. If Judee could cop language from church and put it in a non-church space, then both these spaces must exist. Time must be happening. Duality. Bodies can change. Listening to Bikini Kill taught me to carry knuckle rings, taught me to believe that if I let my body be a woman then at some point I'd be attacked, like being caught in the rain. Listening to Judee Sill taught me that flux and love are real too. I still listen to all these songs.

In Indiana, on the early internet, I found a video of Judee singing her song 'The Kiss'. She sits a piano, her hair heavy and straight. Her face looks like a rodent's and her eyes look beyond. I wanted to sit on a hood in a parking lot and read our horoscopes together. Since she was dead, I researched her life.

Judith Lynn Sill was born in October in Oakland, 1944. Her dad, Milford 'Bun' Sill, owned a farm and imported exotic animals to act in movies. Both he and Judee's brother died in dramatic accidents before she was ten. Her mother, Oneta, remarried, a man who helped animate *Tom and Jerry.* Judee learned to play piano when she was still a kid, and when she was seventeen she married for just a year, to Larry who died taking the Kern River in a rubber raft while he was stoned. Around this time, Judee started robbing banks. The first time she was so nervous she said 'This is a fuckup, mothersticker!' She never hurt anyone with a gun or fists but was caught pretty quickly, and hired a lawyer using her inheritance from her father's death. The lawyer won her extenuating circumstances, so Judee went to reform school instead of jail, where she learned to play religious music and the organ. 'I began to suspect that certain songs evoked certain emotions', she told *Disc and Music Echo.* I felt her. Certain songs I never danced to, ever.

Once free, Judee found work in a saloon, playing the piano. When they found out her age they fired her, and then she took up bass. She married again and her husband, Bob, took heroin so Judee took heroin too. She stopped playing bass, almost died, was caught and arrested again and once she was freed, Judee decided to use 'all the hungry monsters' and become a great songwriter. This to me is the mark of a new life. A new light on an old body. She told *NME* her three main influences were Pythagoras, Bach, and Ray Charles. She always wanted to harmonize with someone but couldn't find anyone, so she decided to do it with the piano instead. With her own voice. From her own body. 'If I could talk about religion', said Judee, 'I wouldn't need to write songs about it'. This was new too: aiming for harmony. I knew *Rip It Up and Start Again,* I knew Chicks on Speed singing about girl monsters, Hedwig Schmidt's surgery, and Wynne Greenwood inventing Nikki and Cola. I hadn't thought about refusing to cut. (Later I read Susan Stryker on Frankenstein and saw Hans Scheirl's *Dandy Dust* and thought again about cutting, but anyway).

Another important part of this story, as I read more and more about Judee, was realizing my life wasn't hers. Our bodies were different. I was trying, am still trying, to figure out mine and mine is not hers. She figured hers out as best she could. Judee wanted to be famous and she talked about being famous in a way that would have been fine if she was a man. But she wasn't, so the newspapers said she was selfish.

Judee Sill was the first album on David Geffen's Asylum label, just before debuts from Jackson Browne and the Eagles. Their successes soon dwarfed hers, financially speaking, but even so she had the cover of *Rolling Stone,* though by then she was talking shit about Geffen. She was falling out of love with Souther. Or maybe she never fell out of love with him. I don't know. 'When I first met Geffen I thought he was some kind of knight in shining armor, you know', Judee said. 'But I didn't understand the other things, the things that made him such a ruthless businessman'. Love and money and bodies. When Asylum released *Heart Food* in 1973, it flopped too.

After that Judee went back and forth from Los Angeles to Mill Valley, she had a car accident and started using heroin again, for the pain, and selling sex to pay for it. A man she picked up at a restaurant on Melrose said they went back to Judee's place and there was a mural-sized portrait of Bela Lugosi, a gigantic ebony cross, and candles everywhere. He says he didn't realize how high she was, right away, but of course they still fucked. Of course he still listened to her read him Aleister Crowley and mystic manuscripts. Here too are bodies, and bright pain at the center. I don't know what happened because I wasn't there. I listen to Bikini Kill and think I know.

Soon this guy said Judee turned into a 'serpentine cadaver', a 'huge gray reptile' curling up on the comforter, and he left her. Which was weak, as Judee wasn't, isn't Medusa. They were just really high. This makes the body shimmer like a song can. When I first heard this story I didn't know to wonder if Judee got off too.

Judee Sill died in a trailer park when she was thirty-five. The night I read that I was alone in my apartment, which had ghosts and a pink-tile bathroom. Maybe it still does. I like trailer parks because people I love live in them. I took *Judee Sill* and hooked it up to my cheap drugstore speakers, which glitter, and I lay on the floor, one speaker face down on my chest. It was half a ritual, but I listened until I fell asleep. Then I woke up and made coffee, and I drank it and I laced up my shoes and left the apartment for work. My life felt a different bright. Like I was living, walking through space after something happened.

4

Lads of Aran

Claire Potter

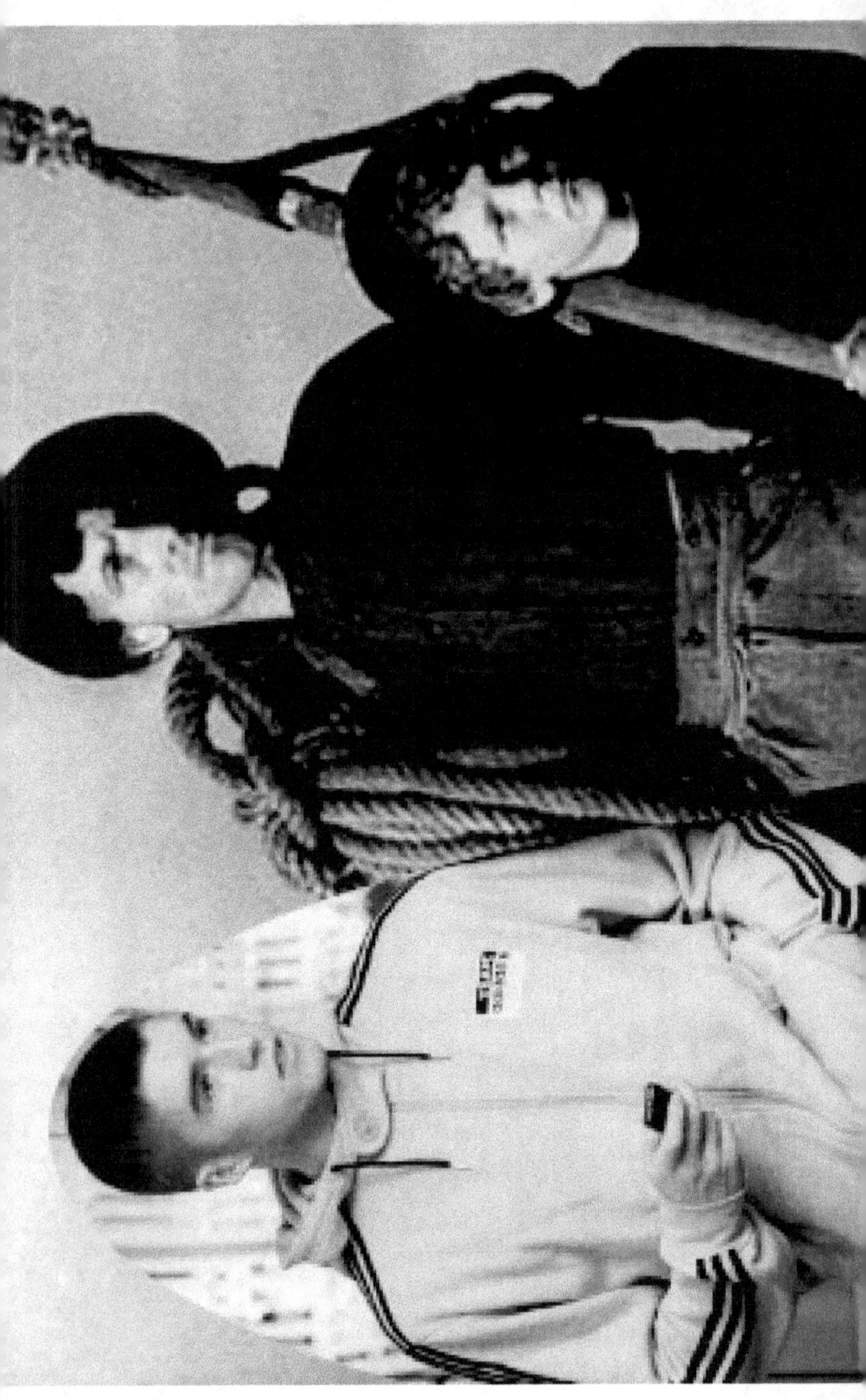

Lads of Aran

1—*Man of Aran* and the Mythic Impulse

'Myths,' writes Claude Lévi-Strauss, 'have one purpose only: to come to terms with **theft**
history, and, on the level of the system, to re-establish a state of equilibrium capable of **of**
acting as a shock absorber for real life events' (1981: 607). Implicit in this formulation is
the idea of myth as an attempt to neutralise history, in that the central goal of the mythic
consciousness is to reduce the complexity of the present by subordinating it to a pattern
established in primordial time. This much is also suggested by Mircea Eliade when he

the polar opposites of one another. Nevertheless, my analysis will show that *Man of
Aran* implicitly encodes a process of cosmological creation, where a deficient cosmology
is transformed into a sufficient one through the actions of man. In detail, this will involve **fire**

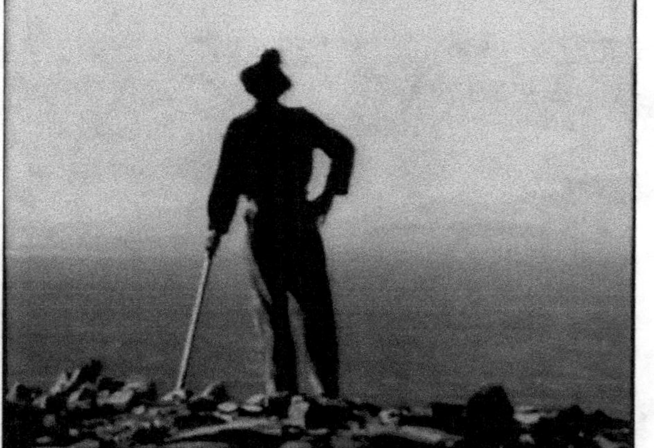

am dead into lads
am interested in   all lads
want to know   all lads
lads in israel known as arsim (male) or
frechot (female)
more accurately translated as pimps
want to know lads on gay sex sites like
councillads.com and
trackielads.org
and I'm all about the Irish collective use:

- Who is having fun on the beach?
- The lads are having fun on the beach—

am bang into nu-lad fashion
as featured in The Guardian in march last year:
style for the post-metrosexual who still drinks cans, likes chips, perfers dogs to cats

am bang into that
want to read it like Barthes' fashion mags
but like; work, masculinity, patriarchy, or cops
and robbers shagging forever.

at base
am interested in myself
(final layer always:
meaningful relation to the world?)
a self-child fucked on a laid down door
another playing big balls, that hermeneutic practice
toward agency, the glorious promise to a child.

when I grow up am being a man
am not being a bird
I'll follow the lads
am being a lad now
will experience fraternity
will know power now
will master postures and the coded exchange
will profit from the given system
will hide fanny in trackies
and trade my way by with pencil-thin spliffs

no doubt, this is what I was saying then
when I didn't know my arse from my elbow but
knew what was what at twelvefourteensixteen now

The land upon which Man
of Aran depends for his
subsistence – potatoes –
has not even soil !

anthropological record. Obviously, different cinematographers will choose to resolve this dilemma in different ways; but there can be little doubt that negotiating a path between the competing imperatives of artistry and accuracy represents perhaps *the* central difficulty of the ethnographic documentary.

coding reside precisely in the *mythic* dimensions of Flaherty's film. In essence, this will involve suggesting that the semantic arrangement of *Man of Aran* made it particularly amenable to the nationalist mythology that informed thinking about the historical emergence of the Irish State. This, I should add, is not to say that Flaherty set out with a

The Allegorical Impulse: Toward

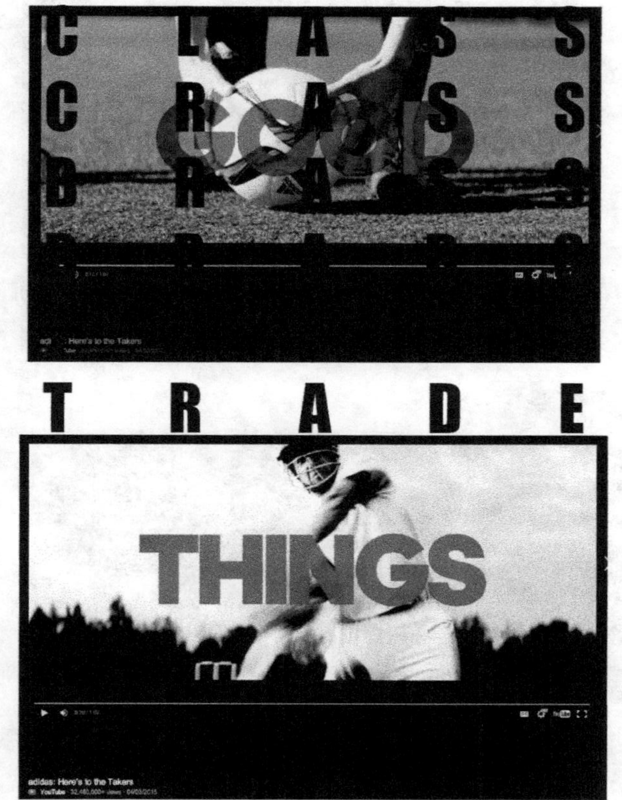

CLASS
CRASS
GOOD
TRADE
THINGS
adidas: Here's to the Takers
YouTube · 32,480,000+ views · 04/03/2015

Triga Films makes gay porn, featuring everything a boy's supposed to want to be;
copper, robber, builder, bouncer, fireman, postman, footballer, fan.

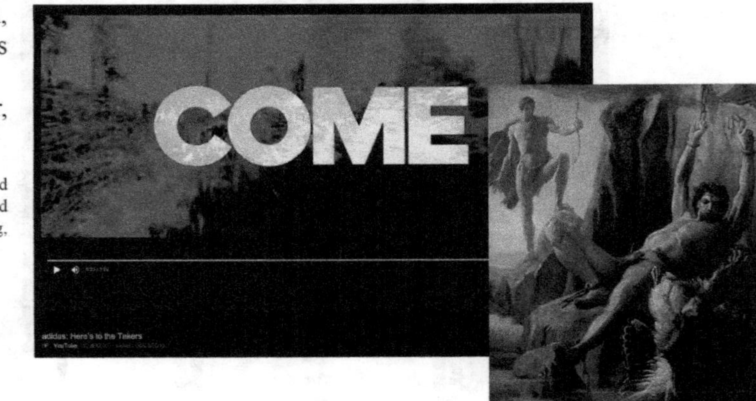

Tinker, tailor, soldier, sailor, rough-handed northern industrial man: economic crisis instead bears the lad. Dolite, trackie-wearing scumbag, drinking
cider in the street
knocking about but
waiting for what?

He's outside the jobcentre
he' outside the shop, sat off
in the beer garden laughing
his bollocks off,
a cig behind his ear.

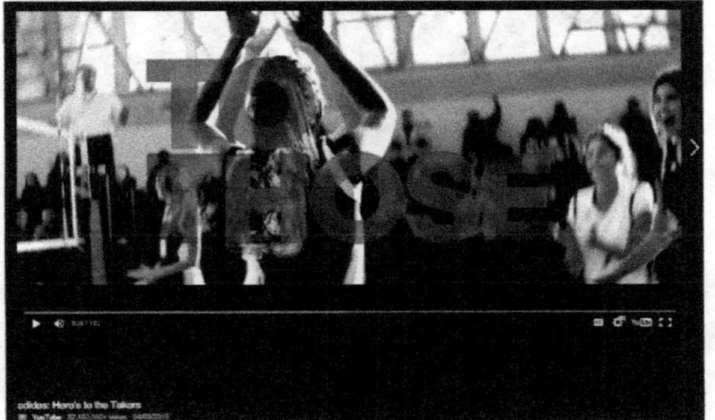

A trailer for a 'grim up north' porn film introduces a lad from a up-tilted angle, the camera's positioned at gut-level for the seated cameraman opposite. The lad sits across the picnic table, answering questions put to him from up and above the film's frame. This viewpoint in conjunction with the Q&A dialogue produces three subject positions: the lad, star of the porn film; the man, camera operator and inquisitor; and the viewer, third party witness (eternally binding by replay). But the slant of this triangulation—an isosceles, where the lad is acute—means the man is able to hold the lad's eye without the camera on the table distracting. And the lad doesn't look down. Engaged as he is deciphering and articulating coded gestures, he doesn't address the viewers. He isn't drawn to the possibility of what is being witnessed and by whom. From that side of the table the triangle is turned. The dual angles are both he and the man.

Man: Unemployed are you lad?
Lad: [Nods.]
Man: Fancy earning yourself a few quid?
Lad: [Laughs.]

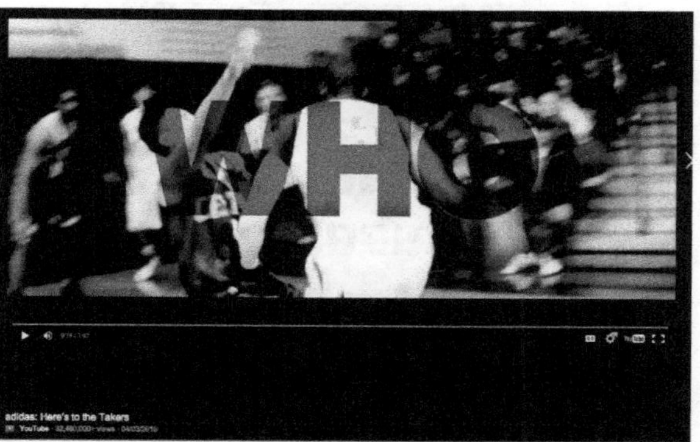

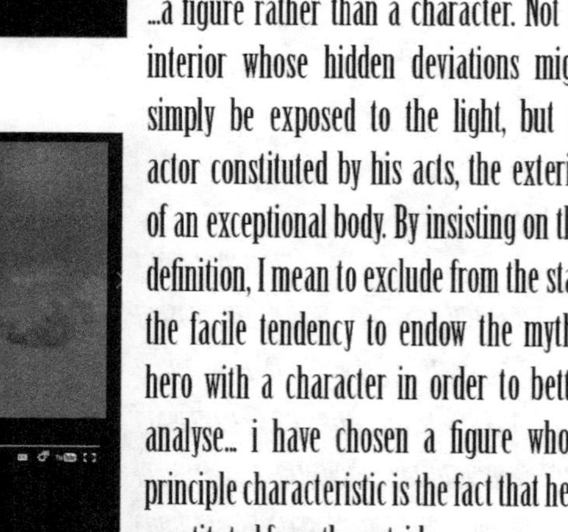

...a figure rather than a character. Not an interior whose hidden deviations might simply be exposed to the light, but an actor constituted by his acts, the exterior of an exceptional body. By insisting on this definition, I mean to exclude from the start the facile tendency to endow the mythic hero with a character in order to better analyse... i have chosen a figure whose principle characteristic is the fact that he is constituted from the outside.

The porn film's conceit is transaction. In the beer garden, the deal is struck that foreshadows a bodily exchange. A verbal contract is tacitly negotiated with reference to employement and the lad is already in debt—he's a pint and a cigarette deep in the man's pocket. But the deal must have already been done, off screen, and it's certainly sealed by the time of watching. The transaction itself is fetishised, the title of the film says so, Straight, Northern and Broke—Extra Taxed! The purchase of labour is affected for our benefit and we role-play witnessing the bond. Always and already contracted by the time of the film's first screening—and don't forget this lad is 'straight'. Renumeration for an employer's use of his body is resolution within this fiction.

Commerce even meant fucking

Active Sports

The Anus and Its Goal-Posts

What you need to do, son is become a fucker and not become a fucked. It's as somple as that. Boys or girls, up the pussy or up the arse, whichever you prefer, but you've got to remember there's a cock betweeen your legs and you're a man.

Colin MacInnes[1]

RUGBY ORGY

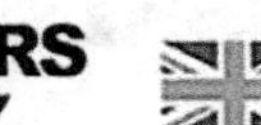

BUILDERS ORGY

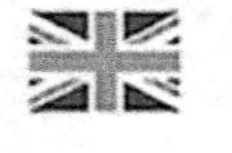

THE POSTMAN ALWAYS FUCKS TWICE: EXTRA TIME

COCKS 'N' ROBBERS

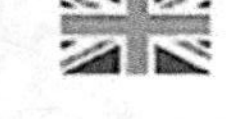
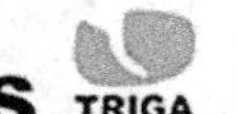

STRAIGHT MARINE BOYS

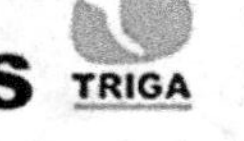

SKINHEADS: STIFF LABOUR

cultural difference, but the adolescent identity is a bricolage. Performances are presented as narrative, ritual and rite. This figure is a ritualised social myth, eokes masculinity to generate social power where there is deficit.

once.

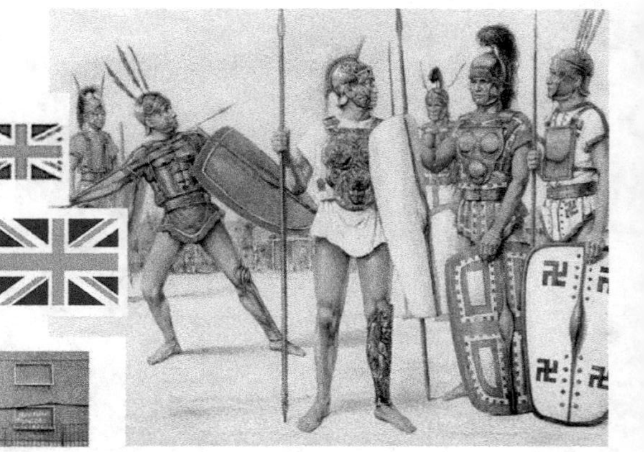

Introduction

Though deserving of its reputation as a masterpiece of ethnographic film-making, Robert Flaherty's 1934 *Man of Aran* reproduces—and indeed initiates—several of the characteristic problems of the anthropological documentary. Primary among these is the

O'Curraidhin (2010) have already produced notable commentaries. Instead, I will suggest that the uncritical valorisation of ethnographic fidelity often forestalls the interpretive

imperative of analysing the ethnographic film as a cultural document in its own right. To that permanent strategy of Western art theory which excludes from the work everything which challenges its determination as the unity of "form" and "content."[32] Conceived as something added or superadded to the work after the fact, allegory will consequently be detachable from it. In this way modernism can

human action is transferred, in *Man of Aran*, to the sea. From this follows not alone the film's mimetic value as an evocation of a maritime culture, but also its aesthetic facility for refracting general truths about human undertakings through a set of local cultural circumstances.

fifteenelevenfourteen went out with a lad called Gaz
had a skinhead he shaved with a Bic razor. He'd
Bic his head in the summer when I was off school
and he was a skiprat or roofy. I'd knock on for him
at his mam and dad's with the brown porch front
on the long road behind a school. I was opening
the door he stepped down on the tiles and yanked the door back shouting what the
fuck do you want, with blood down his face ribboning from the crown, fluid but
still bootstraps. Red drops from his brow screwed up looking at me and my face
told his face that I was scared and he laughed and said only messing you dickhead
and so I laughed too and called him a dickhead too but went in his house.

encodes two contents within one form.[34] Still, the allegorical supplement is not only an addition, but also a replacement. It takes the place of an earlier meaning, which is thereby either effaced or obscured. Because allegory usurps its object it comports within itself a danger, the possibility of perversion: that what is "merely appended" to the work of art be mistaken for its "essence." Hence the vehemence

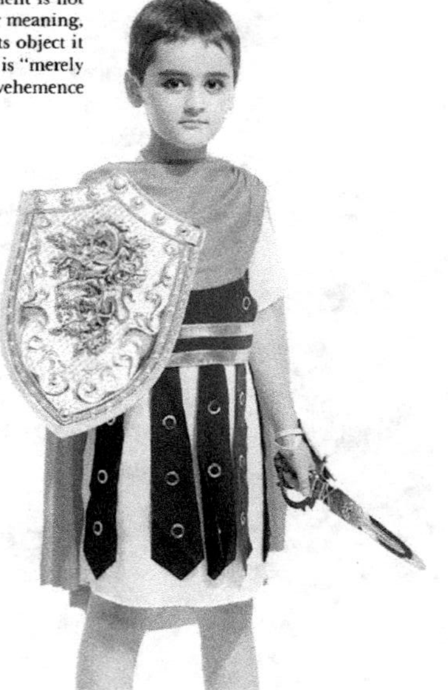

5

Emily Dickinson

Jeremy Millar

About her eyes, and her face, we know the most. It is what we look upon first, look upon most, when we meet someone, it is true, yet such a meeting is for us forever, already, denied. Too late we have come, too early she has left.

About her face I know more than almost anyone else's. At the age of sixteen the length of her mouth crease was 8.5mm; the distance from the edge of her iris to her lower lid was 0.2mm. Is this what we mean by 'know'? Fragments of things, gathered. The distance from her lateral lid crease to upper lid margin was 0.7mm at 3.8mm, in her right eye, and 0.8mm at 3.7mm in her left. Atoms, falling, yet never diminishing that from which they came. The length from her caruncle to lateral canthus? In her right eye, 5.1mm, 4.5mm in her left. Scraps. 'Excuse / Emily and / her Atoms / The North / Star is / of small / fabric but it / implies / much / presides / yet.' How much is implied by, how much authority sits upon, those slant lines of skin? We now know much, and it is always too little.

In perhaps two hundred poems Dickinson made reference to mathematical terms or procedures, often with an exactitude which is lacking in this reference towards them. Counting and measuring figure in many of these, and the reason for such actions is to allow a ratio to be made. For Dickinson this reckoning is most often spiritual, or metaphysical—between Heaven and earth, for example, the unknowable and the known — and emerges from an attentiveness to the tiniest detail. 'I am small,' she wrote, yet for Dickinson 'small' might also mean the North Star.

It is fitting, then, that the measurements we possess of Dickinson's eyes, of her face, were obtained in order that a comparison might be made, between the girl in the daguerreotype of late 1846 — perhaps one made to mark her sixteenth birthday — and the woman in another, made perhaps twelve or thirteen years later.[1] The woman — unlike the girl — is not alone, but is instead seated next to another who is a little older, it seems, although perhaps this is due to a certain gauntness of her face, a thinning of the cheeks, a deepening of the eyes. Yet, even to describe the image invites some confusion, as what we see in the daguerreotype is laterally inverted: we look upon these faces as we would our own, in a mirror. The other woman sits to Dickinson's right, to the right in the image, dark and domed; her clothes perhaps are black, mourning, and brocaded along their edges. White lace crests above her collar. Her hair makes an arch of her forehead, and falls to cover her ears; the pale line of her centre parting leads to an ornate comb which gathers and holds her hair. Her hands rest in her lap, her right bent towards her, her left across it, a ring — or its shadow — just visible upon her middle finger. Her mouth a seabird — a wrinkle in the sky.

To look at Dickinson in this and in the earlier photograph, side by side, is to enact a peculiar, familiar magic. The later dress is almost identical to the earlier one — it might have been cut from the same pattern — and is 'out of date' by period, similar to that which separates them. The hair is parted in the centre, too, although is now slightly looser, and less tight around the ears (the lobe of the left one is higher in both pictures). The lips are full; the cheeks a little fuller. Now her left hand lies across her lap, rather than tipping down from a table edge — now — now — al-

1 This second photograph was discovered in 1995 by a collector known to us as 'Sam Carlo', a pseudonym surely grafted from Samuel Bowles, Dickinson's close friend and probable owner of the daguerrotype, and Carlo, her beloved Newfoundland dog, his name taken from a dog to be found in Jane Eyre; it seems that it is not only Dickinson who is hiding behind this image.

ways the present continuous with a photograph—while the other—the other disappears behind the women next to her, perhaps resting upon her chair or, one hopes, against her back. A thumb stroke—a different tense.[2]

For all that she is presented to us now as an apparition, Dickinson knew all about the changes the body undergoes, its thickening, its thinning, and its decay. In the years following the making of that first portrait, Dickinson suffered numerous episodes of ill health, the symptoms of which—it is likely—would have suggested to her physicians that she was suffering from tuberculosis (TB).[3] Her grandmother, Betsy May Norcross, had succumbed to TB in 1829, the year before Emily's birth; two of Betsy's daughters died of TB, while another, Emily Norcross Dickinson—Emily's mother—displayed symptoms of TB which were described, instead, as 'vague', 'obscure', and 'nameless'. 'It left the little Tint / That never had a Name—'. If the condition was certainly not unknown, then the diagnosis was often left unsaid.

Dickinson's bedroom looked out onto Amherst's West Cemetery, and a quarter of those carried past her window had been consumed by tuberculosis. Many of her early poems place her as both an onlooker and a participant—'It was a short procession— / The Bobolink was there— / An aged Bee addressed us— / And then we knelt in prayer—'; others demonstrate an attentiveness to the body's self-betrayal—such as the frothing of blood at the mouth—and the final, inevitable journey it must then make:

So has a Daisy vanished
From the fields today—

2 It is thought that the second woman is Catherine (Kate) Scott Turner Anthon, with whom Dickinson may have been in love, and who may have been her lover.

3 On Dickinson's probable tuberculosis, and its effect upon those close to her, and upon her poetry, too, I am indebted to George Mamunes' *'So has a Daisy Vanished': Emily Dickinson and Tuberculosis* (Jefferson and London: MacFarland, 2008).

So tiptoed many a slipper
To Paradise away—
Oozed so, in crimson bubbles
Day's departing tide—
Blooming—tripping—flowing—
Are ye then with God?

Death was Dickinson's companion during her youth, yet it was also a possessive one, taking other companions from her, too: 'Death was much of a mob as I could master' she would later write of the period in the early 1850s, when thirty-three young adults in Amherst died, almost all of them from TB. But before this, disease itself can isolate those who act as its host, abusing their hospitality, and in so doing it is not only they who are affected. When Dickinson was only two years old, her mother gave birth to another girl, but took rather a long time to recover. It was decided that Lavinia Norcross, Emily's mother's younger sister, after whom her *own* younger sister was named, would collect Dickinson and have her live with the Norcrosses for a while. While we cannot be certain from what Dickinson's mother was suffering at that time, the disease which spread through the Norcross homestead was far more readily identified. Lavinia Norcross's brother, Hiriam, had died of TB four years previously, and she was now nursing her widowed sister-in-law, Amanda, who was herself in the advanced stages of the disease. The couple had two children, William, and Emily (who later became Dickinson's roommate at Mount Holyoke Seminary); later still they were too amongst the 'daises' mourned by Dickinson, both succumbing, in the early 1850s, to the disease which had killed their parents.

Dickinson's own health was later to become a cause of her isolation, too, albeit more often from her school friends than her family. In 1838, and later in 1844, she missed significant periods of school due to poor health, although this became far worse in the following academic year, when she was able to attend fully for only eleven weeks. As she wrote to a friend, Abiah Root, 'this season is bad for persons who are consumptive.' Even at so tender an age — just fifteen — Dickinson had seen death still the faces of the young, of those denied the opportunity to become old. 'We take no note of Time,' she continued in her letter to Root, 'but from its loss. T'were wise in men to give it then a tongue. Pay no moment but in just purchase of its worth & what it's worth, ask death beds. They can tell.'

Two years later, after Dickinson had entered Mount Holyoke, her cough returned, and in March 1848 her father, Edward Dickinson, was so concerned by this, and her increasingly frailty, that he had her return home. She convalesced there for a month, and probably took a form of opium, before returning to school, fearful of being pitied as an invalid. As she wrote once more to Root: 'I could not bear to leave teaching and companions before the close of term and go home and be dosed and receive the physician daily, and take warm drinks and be condoled with on the state of health in general by all the old ladies in town.' Soon she would have no choice, however, and three months after writing the letter she left the seminary for good, and for her own good, too.

But disease can create a sense of companionship amidst the isolation, too, an experience which can be shared even as it remains resolutely one's own. In early 1865, Dickinson write to 'Cousin Loo', Louise Norcross, that, 'The eyes are as with you, sometimes easy, sometimes worse', thereby suggesting a complaint so familiar to both that it need not be named, and could rest in obscurity. (It is now thought that both suffered from extropia, or deviation of the cornea: a close study of it within the disc of Dickinson's eye in the 1846 daguerrotype shows it to have deviated fifteen degrees from true.)[4] Indeed, obscurity is what was forced upon Dickinson during this period, too, during extended treatments for an eye problem. In both 1864 and 1865 she left the familiarity of not only her home but of Amherst, too, in order that she might travel to Boston to receive treatment

4 On the ongoing problems which Dickinson had with her vision, I am indebted to James R. Guthrie's *Emily Dickinson's Vision: Illness and Identity in her Poetry* (Gainsville: University of Florida Press, 1998).

from Dr. Henry Williams, an eminent ophthalmologist. During this first visit, which lasted seven months, Dickinson was forced to remain in a boarding house amongst strangers, and was further isolated due to Dr. Williams' insistence that she remain in her room; furthermore, she was to lie with her eyes bandaged against the daylight, and could remove them only at sunset, a 'Covered Vision' which would emerge in a later poem. (One presumes that the room's lighting was also suitably dimmed.) Whereas for most of us our eyes first open at the rising of the sun, Dickinson's would at its setting, her day starting as ours might start to end. The rhythms of her day are out of step with that of the sun, and in a number of poems, night and day are exchanged for one another:

> Sunset at Night — is natural —
> But Sunset on the Dawn
> Reverse Nature — Master —
> So Midnight's — due — at Noon.

If in this poem it is as though the mechanics of the universe have broken, a situation which might affect Dickinson, but makes no judgment upon her, another seems to suggest that Dickinson is somehow implicated in the reversal, or may indeed be responsible for it.

> Good Morning — Midnight —
> I'm coming Home —
> Day — got tired of Me —
> How could I — of Him?
>
> Sunshine was a sweet place —
> I liked to stay —
> But Morn — didn't want me — now —
> So — Goodnight — Day!

Dickinson seems to be being punished, here, exiled from the sunshine that she craves. The day tired of her, and the 'Morn' did not want her, yet Dickinson must have been concerned that it was 'Day's Great Progenitor', as she describes God in another poem, who was banishing her from the light. For Dickinson both God and the sun might be considered the same thing — she made use of the felicitous homophone of God the Son/Sun — and she felt God's presence most clearly in the bright light of noon. Here, at its zenith, the sun was closest to heaven, and yet most clearly visible to us, and most clearly illuminating that which surrounds us. At such moments the sun was at its most revelatory, in an optical and a spiritual sense; in revealing our presence upon earth, the sun also lights our way to heaven. Dickinson's communion was, from an early age, defiantly domestic — 'Some keep the Sabbath going to Church — / I keep it, staying at Home —', she wrote in 1852 — and it was within the fourteen acre plot behind the family home that she found her own personal Eden. When her family doctor then prohibited her from visiting it, most especially upon a bright June day, with the sun at its very highest, she must considered this an expulsion from paradise as damning as the original Fall. For what was she being punished? Her refusal to attend church, or to confirm her Christianity during one of the periodic Revivals which spread through New England with a virulence which matched that of another form of consumption? (The two forms are perhaps not unconnected.) Dickinson's consumption was likely tubercular, yes, but it was certainly ocular, and she gathered up her surroundings with her eyes — 'The Meadows — mine — / The Mountains — mine —' — until they could take no more, or were not allowed to, of this heaven on earth. 'Before I got my eye put out / I liked as well to see —', yet perhaps this was not for her to see, or to see yet, and so her sight had to be obscured. If humility is often represented as a lowering of the eyes, then that which God thought to teach Dickinson was achieved through an act rather more violently described.

For Dickinson, her sight was a source of great apprehension: of anxiety, a fearfulness that she might never see again, or read, as she was once prohibited from doing; of capturing and laying claim, as she did upon meadow, and mountain, and 'As much of Noon as I could take'; and of understanding that which surrounded her, even that which — like heaven — might usually be considered to lie beyond our sight. '"How shall you know"? / Consult your Eye!' In time, this last sense took precedence over the first, and Dickinson began to consider her ailment less a punishment than a different form of revelation, one that encouraged the poet to extend her perceptual range. Rather different, scientific examples of such an extension can be found in a number of Dickinson's poems, not least in her ongoing fascination with astronomy, a science that allows one not only to see across vast distances, but also to peer directly into the heavens, and to consider what might be found there.

Dickinson wrote a poem about an astronomer, and used certain technical terms within her work, albeit in ways in which their more usual sense was transformed into something rather more metaphysical — if one might attempt to determine the distance from the earth to the sun, then one might also use means to determine — similarly — one's closeness to God, or alienation, perhaps. During this period such attempts were made using 'parallax', a process by which a distant object is observed from two points, a known distance apart. When the observers attend to the same phenomenon — such as the Transit of Venus across the face of the sun — then difference in angle between their observations can be used to triangulate the distance of the observed object. Is this what we have been doing with Dickinson all along? It is upon Dickinson's face, and not the sun's, that we gaze, and we must do so a little differently. Unable to observe it now — or even at any one time — from two known spatial distances, we must do so instead from distances which are temporal, the 'compound vision' of the photographers' plate cameras, in 1846 and then in 1859, replacing that of the astronomers' telescopes. It is from two different points in time, and not space, that we turn to look upon her, to measure and mark, in the hope that this might also mean to understand. Yet what can we know of her? Like the North Star we might use her to find our way, but she is less constant, or we are. (We most certainly are.) Like the sun, Dickinson marks our days, and yet remains unimaginably distant. It can hurt to look.

'None see God and Live —'

Valeska Gert

TÄNZERIN

6

Pause Between Pauses

Chloé Griffin

There and untenable. Tiny things. Little creepings. Little sounds. Shifting between pauses of dark. Bodies of shadow. Dark light with movement. A night.

Night sounds are like signals reaching outside time. Outside what is tangible. From bodies disappeared into airflows converging again to repeat conversations, dialogues undone, redoing, meeting again.

✡

Is this her grave? Where is it? Valeska Gert, Tänzerin. But there's no date on it… why? Why is there no date on it?

She wanted to have a red coffin... maybe she didn't want a date.

Strange… It's very strange. Like she wants to take herself completely out of time.

She said 'when I'm dead I want to be buried in a cornfield because then the corn grows into my flesh, takes my flesh, and I become bread, no longer dead'.[1]

She thought a lot about this idea of eternity.

This is true, this is true, and she did, yes,

which is essentially what the *Pause* is: taking yourself outside. An impossible idea.

Also what you say about the endlessness, this is not finished... her work is not finished,

and it seems to be exactly what she wanted, what she intended—

like a zombie!

A continuum, a living idea.

She was working with her body really as something different. There's her brain and then her body is really just an instrument to show something else—

to embody the abstract. She wanted to transfigure her body into abstract ideas.

She said, for example, 'I was dancing in 1920 with flickering movements like a film'. Like the flickering light of film—

like traffic, her piece *traffic*—how does *one* body perform traffic?

1 "Ich möchte in einem Kornfeld begraben sein / dann fließt mein Fleisch ins Korn hinein, / dann werd' ich Brot, bin nicht mehr tot." Valeska Gert, *Die Katze von Kampen* (Percha am Starnberger See: Verlag R.S. Schultz 1973), 23.

Yes, yes, in different speeds, in different cars,

in different colors, it's also about thinking — *traffic* —

she doesn't listen to only what the body is saying to do, but she's just looking

how to *embody* traffic, from simply the word.

Different perspectives in one image,

in one body,

in one body, which is given through her body, so her body is just a medium, nothing more.

She goes very far.

Out of range. Outside symbolic borders.

The idea is always this: everything won't fit together but the image you get is also an harmonic image, even if grotesque in a way. Reality is grotesque, it's not harmony.

And her pieces *Baby* or *Death* or the *Procuress,* what you could consider organic realities. Very textual. The dirty body, decay, lust —

she was interested in realism. And she of course saw this also as abstract. But it was always based in realisms and cognitions.

She felt that her piece *Baby* was not kitsch, not expressionist — she felt this was realism.

If you perform a little baby and you are 75 years old, performing it so realistically like she did, of course another effect happens:

mortality.

When was *Baby* written? Did she write it at the same time as *Death*?

I think in the 1920s already, I think *Death* was earlier.

Death was before *Baby*?

Yes. It was art in a way that you take an element from reality and transform it to some other medium, like dance.

She liked to play with people's sensibilities of art. I read that she said she didn't want to have anything to do with art.

Nay, I wouldn't say. Peter Penewski told me that in the 1950s she told him to go to a John Cage exhibition. She was absolutely informed about this modern art, but she was not integrated, she remained outside.

And Günter Brus, from the Vienna Actionism, a very good drawer who did some hardcore performances, says: "then I saw Valeska Gert sitting alone."

One day she gets a letter from Otto Muhl, also a member of this group: "we saw that you performed an orgasm"—but they misunderstand, they want to combine life and reality to bring it into one thing: to make reality into art. And this is not what Valeska did—she just performed. You really see it in *Baby,* when she's finished, she just makes: CUT. Now I'm here, I'm a lady, a 75 year old—not a baby anymore. CUT.

The moment of performance is so intense that it's not sustainable.

You cannot maintain that raw essence without becoming maniacal.

This idea: we open our body and become them by art or by performance.

Art imitates life or life imitates art—

in art you try to open up your real life, something like that—not possible. Bizarre.

Yet Valeska integrated her art into her life by opening these dingey bars[2] and she wrote four autobiographies.[3]

This was her only chance to not become invisible.

She was writing her history.

She said 'Oh these cabaret bars are so boring'. So she performed the KZ commander Ilsa Koch.

Who was going there?

She said all the men from Judy Garland...

All the men of Judy?

Her husband and all the immigrants from Europe from the 1920s, 1930s—Dada artists. She said that Tennessee Williams was working there as a server and that he was stealing money, so she kicked him out. And this seemed so typical Valeska. She wasn't really angry; she just said "he was cheating me with money so I kicked him out."

I read that she thought The Beggars Bar was her jungle, that she was like a hunter.

---

2 *Der Kohlkopp* (Berlin, 1932); *Die Bettler Bar* (West Village, NYC, 1941); *Café Valeska und ihr Kuchenpersonal* (Zurich, 1946); *Die Hexenkuche* (Berlin, 1950); *Der Zeigenstall* (Kampen, 1951).

3 *Mein Weg* (1931); *Die Bettler Bar von New York* (1950); *Ich bin eine Hexe* (1968); *Katze von Kampen* (1973).

Yes, and Jackson Pollock was in her bar—a lot of interesting people. If you create a space with a special spirit, people come to you, you don't have to invite them to your home, you make a public place.

Do you think she needed the attention?

Yes, yes, but afterwards it was more of a production space. She asked other people to perform. She would blow them up, she would pump them up full of air, because she has a talent—not to manipulate—but to make people look very interesting. There is a picture of a beautiful girl walking through the bar holding a candle and a bottle and it's called *Candle Dance*. I mean imagine: 1950, a girl going across the stage and making a *candle dance*—very subculture, very modern.

Do you think being outside enabled her to be instinctual with her ideas—to arrive at these visionary points?

I would say she was a visionary because she has good intuition to where borders are. She always feels new borders. And she is absolutely perfect to see through these things. Like a Rückblick. A backward glance. She really has a look. In the 1950s, during the trial against this Nazi woman, Ilsa Koch, she makes a performance that integrates this person, a woman in the '50s, like "oh I'm just a little knitting woman, I'm just a housewife." She integrates this normality, and makes it even more grotesque. What Valeska shows in her performance is that this woman—this Nazi—is not full of lies, she's just full of Widerspruch. Of contradictions. Things not fitting together. But for this woman, this is normal. She feels totally normal. She does not see herself as a monster, she thinks she's a nice person.

She's like multiples of a presence.

Valeska is more than one time here: she is three times here.

Interesting, the borders. She uses her body in different tenses of time. Takes it as a means of possession. Bodily? Borders to possess.

We don't know where the borders of our bodies are. You know this experiment with the two fingers: you touch your finger with mine and then feel them together. You can't tell where I start and where you start. So you don't know where the borders of your own body are really, you get totally confused. You don't know where borders start, and where they end. These are Valeska's experiments. The physical things she works with.

For example she said—as I remember—"I was going down on my knees, the dance was called *Sprung,* like the Olympic game 'Leap'. I was on my knees and I started looking at the audience longer and longer, because so light no jump can be, which is a jump only existing in your brain."

To transform this dynamic action into the abstract liberates it into an endless, bodiless space.

And this idea of a *pause,* of *time.* Not *death,* but *pause,* which is time made static — still motion. Like death, but different — an anticipated tense meant to resume. A true form of the abstract.

A *pause* doesn't even exist. Pause is complete concept.

You don't know the end and you don't know the beginning. And you know that a pause has to have borders, in the beginning and the end. A *pause* has to have an end, without an end it is not a pause anymore.

You take *time,* already an abstract, and then you take something (a fragment) inside there.

What was the premise for that piece?

She said that Bertolt Brecht discovered her while she was performing the *Pause* between pauses in films, when they changed the film rolls.

I like the way you just said she performed the *Pause* between pauses.

No. I don't know if she did the *Pause* piece in the pause.

Oh. What?

I have only a book where you see a lot of dances with titles and one title is *Pause.* Most dances are known, like *Nervosität,* and then there's this one dance: *Pause*—but there's no description.

So in a sense this concept is yours as well as Valeska's?

Yes, like Marcel Duchamp's urinal, there is no original existing; it's just from a photo. The book is about dance from 1923 or something. Nobody talked about this modernity. The book came out with photos and titles. Nobody talked about it. Just like nobody talked about the ready-mades until the '60s when Andy Warhol said this was amazing, and then they reproduced the urinals. Nobody taped these performances and no urinals were left, only a cup. No original ready-mades were left, all were remade, only the photos existed from the original.

These things are so ephemeral. It's really about challenging the imagination of the future. And this really connects with her because she was so fascinated by the future.

She wanted to live when she is dead.

Yes this fits. But I wasn't the first to discover it. Susanne Foellmer, a dance scientist who comes from the feminist movement, wrote in her book—a very good book, very scientific book—that Valeska also danced perceptions of slow motion, of film, elements of new aesthetics, new techniques, also the *Pause.* Susanne described something really different, because the men always described Valeska as dancing the prostitute, the wet-nurse, the birth giving, so you really see a very different view from Susanne Foellmer, a feministic view. She's German.

Was she one of the first to write about Valeska in Germany?

She was the first to focus on Valeska and compare her to other women in art, really good artists. She was the first to bring her out of the cabaret,

out of the Weimar,

and bring her to the modern. Like Marcel Duchamp's urinal—it's just the gesture, it's just the decision

—the moment of jumping off.

And now I'm writing a book about the *Pause*. And there are other scientists that have made ideas of *Pause*. I think this is an open space, everyone can use her—this is absolutely in the sense that she wanted. Nobody can say *Pause* is mine.

Transfiguring her body into *Pause* enables a borderless becoming. Flesh to corn to bread. And the idea of *pause* is an untenable thing in its very essence.

And here is an example, a new interpretation of the *Pause* by Philipp Gutbrod: the body shape of Valeska in the *Pause* looks similar to the viertelpause—the quarter rest—the symbol of the musical notation of the pause. That this could be the reason for giving the image the title *Pause*.

It's so interesting that these dances exist only in pictures now. They're static—but void of movement. It reminds me of her piece *Sprung—The Leap*—in that performance, it is as if she stays in the photograph, in the position from which the imagination now goes… you can't take it further.

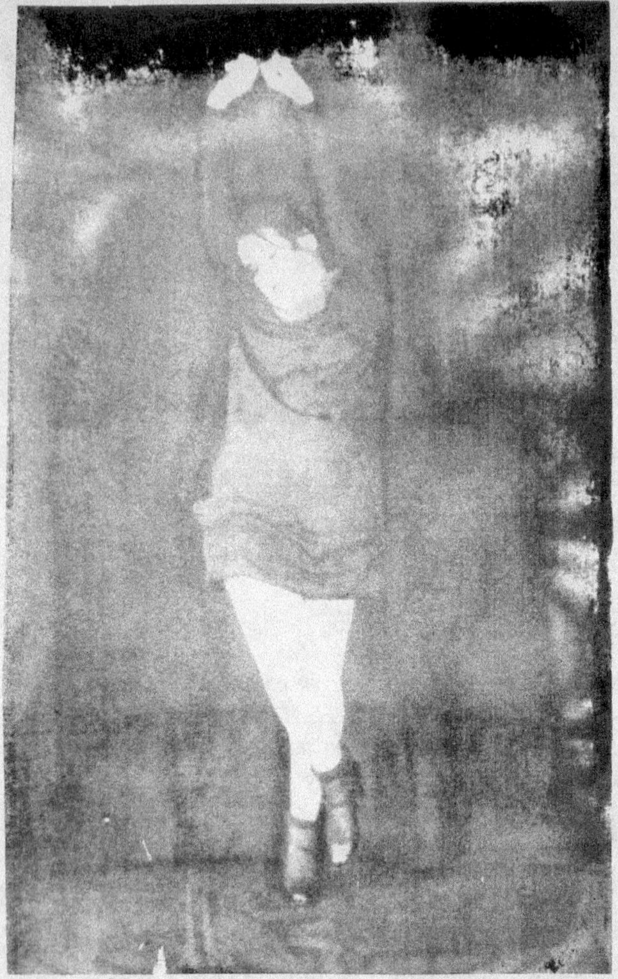

Pause.

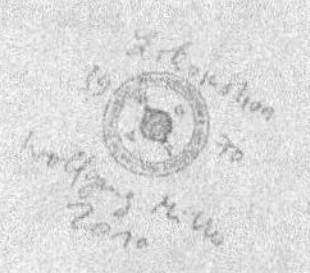

She says 'my main intention for my dances is shortness and simpleness of form. Clear. Kurzes und einfachheit.'

I like how this *shortness* or *briefness* relates back to the tense nature of a *pause*. And also to the structure, space and process of the body. Like briefness exemplifying these mortal bones in relation to the elements around us. And simplicity: just this traceable body boundary. Unlike a painter or writer, she uses simply her own temporal body.

I think she understood that if you combine three or four things in the same moment, things which are not fitting together, you become full of life and endless. And this she understood. Most actors think 'I must fulfill this role, play this ugly or this evil one...' and she understood that you open space if you are not so in one direction, but also a step to the right and left and backwards. Therefore her performances were recognized as full of life.

Then it's a continuum, a living idea,

like a zombie!

And it seems to be exactly what she wanted, what she intended.

Also what you say about the endlessness, this is not finished... her work is not finished.

Which is essentially what the *Pause* is… taking yourself outside. An impossible idea.

This is true, this is true, and she did, yes.

I read that she thought a lot about this idea of eternity.

She said 'when I'm dead I want to be buried in a cornfield because then the corn grows into my flesh, takes my flesh, and I become bread, no longer dead'.

Strange. It's very strange. Like she wants to take herself completely out of time.

she wanted to have a red coffin... maybe she didn't want a date.

✡

Why do we need bodies? Around our selves — this other whirling of mass — blood, water, air and other things: brackets, boundaries, beautiful limitations. Pressings. Red coffins. Our bodies and — the *Pause* — between our bodies. Next decay.

The *Pause* —

a soul

between beginning and end. A body's end. The finishing of our red mass material. What finish? To dirt? Into the passage of some other finishing? And then?

The *Pause* —

again

outside time — (inside). To take on the eternity.
To *embody*

Endlessness.

✡

This text is conceived from a conversation between Chloé Griffin and Wolfgang Müller one evening in Berlin. October, 2015.

✡

Valeska Gert was born in Berlin in 1892. She was a German Jewish dancer, actress, and avant-garde performance artist.

In 1938 she emigrated to New York city, where in 1941 she opened The Beggars Bar in the West Village. In 1947 she returned to Europe and a blockaded Berlin.

In the 1960s and '70s she appeared in films by directors Federico Fellini, Rainer Maria Fassbinder and Volker Schlondorff. In 1978 she was invited to play in Werner Herzog's remake of *Nosferatu* but died 10 days before the shooting on March 16th.

Wolfgang Müller is a Berlin artist, musician and author. He founded the multi-media performance art group *Die Tödliche Doris* (active 1980–1987) and has published numerous books, including most recently *Subkultur Westberlin 1979–1989* (Fundus, 2014).

7

Brigid Brophy

Phoebe Blatton

In talking about death, numbers matter immensely. Dates matter; the date illness was first recorded, dates marking the decline, the date of departure, the date that will come round again as the years roll on, reiterating the shock of death however well it was expected or not. Age matters, supposedly to a greater of lesser extent depending on the age at the time of death. The time of death, that point at which our mattering is blown apart, scattered to the soil of a time beyond us where it'll either bury down into this-or-that subjective or objective meaning or simply evaporate, is recorded, to keep hold of things, to make things 'sensical'; an adjective that doesn't officially exist because 'sense' has multiple meanings, unlike its 'nonsensical' antonym. But language doesn't abide, it writhes against logic, through logic, creates its own. Language can describe death, but only from the outside. Numbers don't explain, but they delineate death, and they continue where we don't.

I had my first encounter with the novelist, playwright, critic and campaigner Brigid Brophy, aged nineteen, in a book of collected texts celebrating women's fiction from every year of the Twentieth Century. The collection featured an extract of Brophy's 1956 novel, *The King of a Rainy Country,* and a short biography, stating that she had died in 1995, five years prior to the compilation's publication. It is not remarkable to find out that a writer, though new to you and surely a source of further wonder, is dead. But it is strange and saddening to know they might still have been alive and writing should they not have been, as people say, 'taken too soon'. Brigid Brophy died at only 66 years of age.

Excited by the aforementioned extract, I bought a second-hand copy of *The King of a Rainy Country* on the Internet, as it was very much out of print at that time. It has affected my life like no other novel, not only because of how I identified with the intangible school experience of the central character, Susan, as she fell in love with fellow pupil Cynthia, or because in Brophy's voice I heard a spectrum of musings on gender deftly issued before such studies on the subject were established, the future reborn in her clear, yet ever-tantalising prose. For these reasons, I found myself angry that it was out of print, angry once more at the howling omissions of writers such as Brophy from the predominantly male canon of Twentieth Century English Literature. Angry that writers like her were dismissed in her time as 'oddties' or merely 'fashionable' when in fact they were unashamedly progressive and 'other', thus writing the experience of many. I realised that I and a good set of friends might have to be the people to re-publish *The King of a Rainy Country,* and reintroduce Brigid Brophy to a new audience. As a result of this endeavour, I find myself, in all humbleness, associated with her name. All because I had once so strongly associated with this 'cut-down version' of herself, as she once described Susan, in a rare concession to the autobiographical.

Brophy was staunchly 'un-autobiographical', as she touched upon in the essay *Antonia* for the 1987 re-issue of her novel, *The Finishing Touch.* Therefore, an essay written one year earlier in 1986, was surely a concession of even greater rarity than the fictional offering made in *The King of a Rainy Country.* The essay, commissioned for the American Contemporary Authors Autobiography Series, and later published in Brophy's collection of non-fiction, *Baroque n' Roll,* is written in 20 short sections, and called *A Case-Historical Fragment of Autobiography.* The scrupulous detail and phrasing almost surpasses that which we might call 'typically Brophean', telling of how Brophy had lived and worked for the past four years under the degenerative, humiliating and surreal effects of what was for two years, a mystery condition. With each section, she systematically logs the progress of events and investigations that led to her diagnosis, in 1984, of Multiple Sclerosis.

Over the years I have collected books and ephemera that have passed through Brophy's own hands, often bearing her inscriptions. One of these items is a proof copy of Patricia Highsmith's psychological thriller *This Sweet Sickness* (1960), with Brophy's keen reviewer's notes in the margins. The book, as one would expect, is a no-frills paperback proof; musty smelling, with an age-spotted blue-and-white striped cover that had not yet been assigned a final design. It is an exciting object because it represents a connection between two writers I consider my 'greats', and is tactile evidence that Brophy, like myself, was a great admirer of Highsmith. This, I can only conjecture to an extent from the object, though I have heard two accounts of meetings between the women. The first was from the writer and Brophy's long-time partner, Maureen Duffy. She told me about driving Brigid to Switzerland to meet Pat, only to arrive at the reclusive writer's fortress of a house, with Brigid cowering in the backseat in a rare show of nerves. Maureen conjured a vivid image of the formidable Pat sauntering towards the car, as though she might reach in through the half-open window, like a murderer from one of her novels, and strangle the naïve intruders. Nevertheless, Patricia Highsmith was famously awkward in her physical carriage. Kate Levey, Brophy's daughter, told me that 'Writers both, Brigid and Pat had in common a profound shyness about face- to- face meetings.' In Andrew Wilson's biography of Highsmith, the writer's rigidity and discomfort in her own body is illustrated in an anecdote from Barbara Roett: 'I always remember that she was quite shocked when I once said, "I must go lie down in a bath." She'd never actually laid down in a bath.'

It is Kate Levey who provided the second story- a childhood memory of being off school sick, and, for want of her mother finding a babysitter, reluctantly taken to lunch at a Chinese restaurant in Earl's Court. Brophy had an unmissable date with Patricia Highsmith. 'That Pat had flown in from somewhere that morning struck me, in itself, as exciting and odd,' said Kate, 'but then the whole occasion was strange. Pat seemed large and rather severe.' Highsmith, though clearly the subject of her mother's awe, unnerved the young Kate, especially when she opened the fold of her jacket to reveal a jar of live snails that she'd smuggled into England (fables surround Highsmith and her pet snails, which she purportedly often transported in her bra). Some mild teasing ensued, with suggestions of the chefs getting hold of these snails for the menu. 'Pat's pet snails were not as troubling to me as the thought that she'd done something illegal, rigidly righteous child that I was.' An air of illegality was surely part of what drew the two women to each other, both acutely non-hetero, attuned to perversity, and always worrying at the boundaries of conventional behaviour through their writing and their bodily experiences of the worlds in which they lived.

The proof copy of *This Sweet Sickness* is not something I look at often. I bought it during a period of time working at a second-hand bookshop on Charing Cross Road, where I witnessed the nerdy fetishism of collecting rare books. The majority of the collectors were male, mostly the sort that revel in a kind of 'out of society' existence that is maddeningly the privilege of men, and which expresses itself across a spectrum of behaviour from not washing to blatant sexism, albeit of an often 'vintage' kind. This prevalent image was highly influential in my dislike of book collecting, but I admit to sometimes being seduced by the seemingly magical, transmissive properties of first editions and signed copies of books by the authors I love. It was during this time that I picked up the proof, which as the stories above concur, is *proof* of another kind. There is a line that leads from the flecks of pencil in Brophy's own hand to an imagining of her body, hunched into the warm back-seat of a well travelled car, or to her pushing open the door of a busy Chinese restaurant with her child's sweaty, reluctant paw pressed into her other hand, releasing it as she goes to embrace, with surely some excitement and trepidation, the daunting, unyielding body of Patricia Highsmith.

What is it about, this imagining of Brophy as 'a real person'? Perhaps it is the sensation one has of reading her novels — and I think it specifically applies to novels for their immersive, long-form — as a young person, that seems so pointedly to have touched the core of what you feel before you have the words or experience to express it, and propels you onto a whole new plateau of experiencing the world. Like a love affair, it has made you think completely differently and broken your heart a little. The writer has helped you, in a profound way, to exist. It feels impossible that it is the work of a stranger.

A dedication from Brigid Brophy, in the First Edition I own of *Baroque n' Roll,* reads 'This copy, belonging to Geoff Napthene, is inscribed with best wishes to him by Brigid Brophy. London, June 1987'. You could say that the opening essay, *A Case-Historical Fragment of Autobiography,* about her life with Multiple Sclerosis, has in fact begun in the dedication to Geoff, penned in blue ink. It's not that the dedication has any connected meaning, rather that her stylish handwriting, lithe characters evoking the typographies of Art Nouveau, do not look quite as they appeared in the margins of my copy of *This Sweet Sickness.* Words take drunken dips and letters lurch away from each other. 'O's compress, and 'i's are stranded. Here is proof, of a less romantic kind this time. Proof that Brophy's body was in decline.

✲

It was recently revealed that Brigid Brophy and Iris Murdoch exchanged thousands of letters over their lifetimes. On strict orders from Brigid, every letter to Iris was burnt, so we shall only ever see the evidence of Murdoch's hand, and the nature of her responses (often surprisingly subordinate and deferential, as might befit the dynamic of a relationship that surpassed the platonic) to guess at the content of Brophy's letters. I wonder if those letters, like my copy of *Baroque n' Roll,* had become depressing visual clues as to the state of Brophy's health. One can imagine her physical decline showing on the page, while – cruel irony – the parallel decline of her friend's mind into Alzheimer's disease might also have begun to show in their meetings and exchanges. Iris Murdoch features in *A Case-Historical Fragment,* having met Brigid for lunch in the New Year of 1984 at a restaurant that could only offer them a table up a flight of stairs. 'Iris robustly put her hand beneath my elbow and hoisted me up it,' she simply notes, with no further elaboration on the more famous writer, or the old affair that was to become public knowledge years after their deaths. In retrospect, that sentence in isolation contains an elegy to something far greater, more physically and emotionally entwined, than the moment in which a hand held an elbow.

A catalogue of relationships with women emerge in even a brief consideration of Brophy's life. She was rarely without a passionate attachment to a woman, despite her marriage to the art historian and Director of the National Gallery, Michael Levey. She accepted his proposal of marriage with the caution that, 'Until a year or so ago I was at least 50% homosexual, and this was the half I acted upon.' Their marriage, however, was strong. A love absolute, but neither owned each others' hearts exclusively, nor seemingly wished to. Brophy, a self-professed 'natural egalitarian' and so progressive in her writing and left-wing thinking, could no more limit her ideas about sex and bodies, as evidenced in her campaign for Sex Education, than her writings on the rights of all sentient beings — fish included — which led to her veganism and anti-vivisectionist stance. Indeed, she acknowledges that her illness gave her 'a stake in the matter' of vivisection. 'What is the life of this rat or the freedom from terror and agony of that monkey worth to us?' was a question she thought not-to-the-point. 'The pertinent question,' she replies, 'is what they are worth to that monkey or this rat. His life is the only one that is open to him. His awareness, which you can so easily suffuse with torment, is the only one he can experience.' Shocked into bodily awareness and reckoning with mortality, she continued to live according to logic, and would refuse any treatment that had benefited from the 'fascist atrocity' she regarded as vivisection.

It seems that on beginning *A Case-Historical Fragment of Autobiography,* the surprise severing of a particularly important relationship might be regarded as the 'catastrophic grief' that triggered her illness. Within the first paragraph we are offered a relay of psychological *ambushes, trembles and tumbles,* by an unnamed 'assailant' who resonates deep into the essay as they manifest in Brophy's flesh. In true equivocal fashion, she simply orchestrates our feeling on the subject, by placing the event in the first section of the essay, of which, as I have mentioned, there are twenty. According to her values, it is with the 'automated version of a formal logician' (the computer) that she believes the causes of Multiple Sclerosis will and should be deciphered, with a catalogue of data that involves much questioning of the patients. Nevertheless, frequent mentions of the 'assailant' who maims her in her nightmares, are indication of a fallible, angry Brophy, in battle with reason and rationality. One can only speculate if wounds of the heart were salted by the physical wounding of her disease. In the end, there is a kind of amnesty of logic, and of vengeful suggestion. As though in surrender to the surreal nature of her condition, she leaves it until the seventeenth section to concede that 'the question of what does induce it [multiple sclerosis] may well drop out of the accumulated and sifted replies to a question as seemingly wayward as "Do you like blackcurrents?"'

Following her logical dismissal of mysterious forces, she writes; 'If it is random bad luck to be struck down by the disease, it is random comparatively good luck to be struck down in a welfare state.' It is a taught, deftly balanced sentence in which the devastation of being 'struck down' is immediately cloaked in a 'bigger issue'; a neater example of 'the personal is political' is hard to find, and it clearly places Brophy on the Left. It is arguably a sentence with even greater prescience today. Welfare state or not, it is worth considering the privileges Brophy might have experienced as a sick woman of a particular class and ethnicity. Brophy mentions how her husband wrote to the head of the unit at the hospital in which she was being treated when there was a mix up with her appointments. There's little doubt that a letter from the recently knighted Director of the National Gallery would have carried some clout. Perhaps it is tangential to here cite the case of Afro-German poet, activist and educator, May Ayim, who committed suicide in 1996 at the age of thirty six, but I believe it is in the spirit of Brophy to do so. Though very different writers, who lead very different lives, there are points of comparison between the women, notably their activism, and their contraction of multiple sclerosis. May Ayim had been admitted to the psychiatric ward in Berlin in January 1996, shortly after a strenuous period organising Black History Month. The doctors eventually diagnosed her as having multiple sclerosis. They stopped her medication, which had been based on believing she had severe depression, and discharged her in April. Following subsequent readmission and release from the hospital, on August 9th she jumped from the thirteenth floor of a Berlin building. In the case of any suicide, the question of whether it could have been prevented is always difficult to answer, but on hearing this story I was struck by the apparent failure of care surrounding Ayim's depression and multiple sclerosis; illnesses that might not have been unrelated. I doubt that Ayim would have come across Brophy's essay on multiple sclerosis in the few months between her diagnosis and death, but if she had, would she have recognised the 'obsessive and fearful state of mind' that Brophy experienced before her diagnosis, interpreted as 'imitations from my body [that] were alerting my mind to facts it did not know'? It is for another essay to go deeper into the various issues surrounding the death of May Ayim, which are surely located in an endemically racist system, but I am sure that both writers would want us to think about how two people from First

World countries with the same disease, might well have received different 'treatment' according to the bodies they inhabited.

✡

Where it could seem quite odd, in an essay that is ostensibly about her reckoning with a slow, surreal illness, to encounter one section given over to the details of the Public Lending Right (the campaign that Brophy and Maureen Duffy spearheaded to ensure writers were paid for their inclusion in public libraries), in Brophy's hands, this diversion into a relatively unexciting though significant enterprise is integral to the emotional head-spin that we experience by the end of the essay. It is because she enjoyed the 'mechanical and relaxed delight' of logic, 'which served me as, I imagine, knitting serves some of my friends', that she came to embrace and enjoy her immersion into the rules of British Copyright.

The essay is at times infuriating, because it is so controlled, so seemingly sat bolt-upright in a bath full of murky water. Brophy writes with a kind of pedantry that at times reads like the reporting of a ponderous Police Detective. But it is inclusive, talking us through the 'intellectual knitting', she could so enjoyably lose herself in when presented with puzzles in the minutiae. The disease that had so ravished her was, of course, a puzzle that she knew she would fail to solve. The essay often reads like an attempt to exercise control, the twenty sections resembling 'steps', like the literal steps she has to take with extreme effort. Before the illness is diagnosed, we hear of how Brophy would scale the six steps of the minor portico that led to the communal front door of her building. After heaving herself up via the railings, 'I crawled on all fours through the communal hall, wondering whether the occupant of some other flat would at that moment come down the staircase or, having begun to do so, would retreat thinking "There's that eccentric Lady Levey crawling across the hall"'.

Never does she let the tragedy of her illness fully erase the humour and sense of the surreal that so colours and defines her writing.

In the twentieth section of the essay, Brophy concludes with a typically equivocal segue into a memory of standing on the 'wind-racked grass at the top of the site of Troy. To one side were the quasi-terraces cut by the excavation to disclose the layers of the successive cities.' She is there with two companions, one of which we might assume to be her husband, and the other Maureen Duffy, though she does not say. The important thing is that they are three, and are approached by three local children, 'seriously beautiful, and without a touch of the urchin, seriously serious', bearing long-stalked, vermillion poppies. The scene ripples with an earthy, magical atmosphere that one might associate with Fellini. Indeed, it is as though the whole scene might suddenly melt like celluloid and disappear into its own oblivion. At the very last, she reveals a kind of writing that conveys the surreality of her condition, that choruses that experience of a 'strange, unnatural numbness', lying in bed at night and not being able to 'tell whether I have crossed one ankle over the other unless I look to see.' Brophy does not write about flowers without knowledge of their symbolism, and in the myths of Ancient Greece, poppies were used as offerings to the dead. Recognising this courtesy as an act of 'high Homeric custom', Brophy searches for something to offer in response. In her pockets she has a clutch of boiled sweets that she describes as 'big cellophane-swathed ovals in the deep, not quite transparent colours of jewels'. Having created this upward arc of poetic description, in the next moment we are adroitly brought over the peak and into the decline with a knowing, yet poignant admission of the absurd; 'I am the ancient Greek ghost, sent down in the ultimate sense, who on meeting Charon proffered a boiled sweet as the price of the ferry passage.'

The children did not accept the sweets, a sign perhaps that at that moment she had not been deemed 'unfit' enough to make the passage. Yet writing in 1986, she knows that 'all that has happened to me is that I have in part died in advance of the total event.' Brophy expresses her losses physically, through the body. The knowledge that she will never see Italy again is described as 'an unbearable medallion that bends my neck'. She describes the past as ' except through memory and imagination, irrecoverable in any case, whether or not your legs are strong enough to sprint after it.' Perhaps the recollection of the children of Troy is her way of saying that the future, her present, was ever thus, and she will attempt to accept it.

The coincidence of numbers strike me again. *A Case-Historical Fragment of Autobiography,* written in twenty short sections, is really the whole of everything you need to know about Brophy, though she will challenge you, like the excavators of Troy, to 'disclose the layers'. It is now twenty one years since Brigid Brophy died. Last year, on the twentieth anniversary of her death, the University of Northampton arranged a conference to celebrate her life, to which I was invited to talk about publishing *The King of a Rainy Country.* When I talk about the novel, I celebrate how it achieves nothing so ill-conceived or presumptuously linear as a point of enlightenment, but rather illustrates what it is to merely glean the shimmer of that which is intangible. We speak of losing someone as 'an intangible loss', meaning the grief caused by their absence is too great to quantify. The intangible loss I feel for Brophy is rather more literal, because of course, though having grown close to those who knew her, in particular her daughter Kate, I never did.

Could it be that an 'intangible loss' is as intangible as the love that prefigured it?

At the end of *The King of a Rainy Country,* Susan learns of the death of Helena, a friend, though that word falters in its reach, that she has only just made. I have since been told that Helena might well have been named after a girl called Helen, who Brophy knew at Oxford, from which Brophy was 'sent down' for 'unspecified offences', and who had been killed. Brophy writes as someone who completely understands the way in which trauma does not necessarily erupt immediately, but quakes from the inside. Perhaps this especially applies to the experience of those who have had to live and love as 'other', and more often than not, with shame. When Susan learns of the death of her friend, there is no 'normal response'. She is gripped by the sudden, inexplicable urge to call her dentist.

I asked if I could have an appointment at once.

'Is it urgent? Are you in actual pain?'

'No. That's the trouble.'

'I don't quite see what you mean.'

Brophy wrote *The King of a Rainy Country* at the age of twenty seven. Until her diagnosis with multiple sclerosis she had only experienced exceptionally good health. Nevertheless, these lines of Brophy's, delivered in the voice of her semi-autobiographical, nineteen-year-old Susan, reveal a woman who had always faced the intangible, proffering her sweets.

'I haven't been for some time.' Susan tells the receptionist, a kind of Charon of the Dentist's chair.

'There's bound to be something that needs doing, isn't there?"

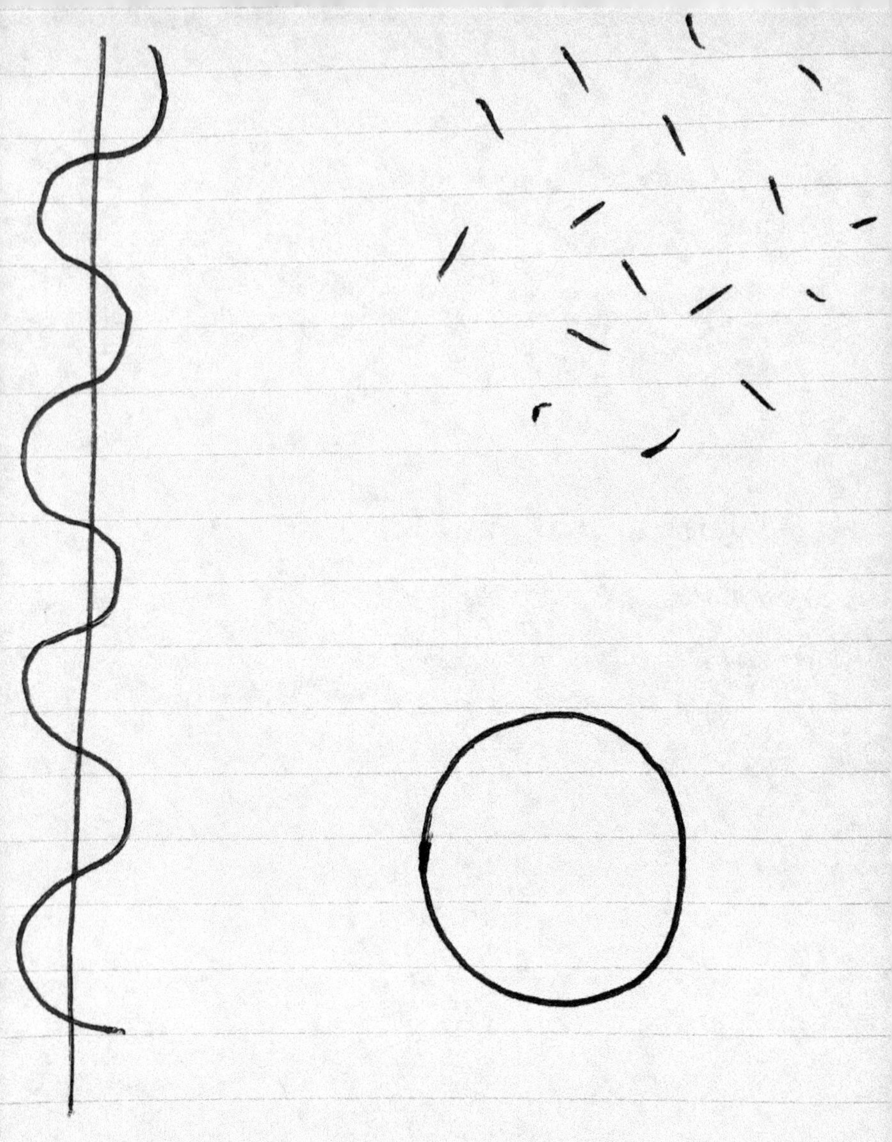

Fragment: Memory of structures. Blasted. Cleansed. Crave. 4:48. The writer mimics her markings. Clasps them in comfort. "I asked her again about *4:48 Psychosis* and the form she was striving to create. She grabbed a piece of file paper from my desk and drew another diagram. She reiterated the *Cleansed* diagram - the straight line being the plot and the wavy line the story. Then she drew another diagram for *4:48 Psychosis.* The circle is the story and, to the right, entirely separate from it, is the plot: a series of disconnected atomic fragments. The analogy was with the self, experienced in bits, unprotected by any coherent sense of whole personality, opened fatally to the world." Dan Rebellato, 'Sarah Kane Interview', *Dan Rebellato* (blog), 3 November 1998, http://www.danrebellato.co.uk/sarah-kane-interview/.

8

A Body. Beat.

Susanna Davies-Crook

Dull thud of
endings. Nerve sparks
Can't think
Imaging you
A forward motion. A swirl and stomach clench sick fall face
first. Fucked.
Calm is for lives. Windows blind,
curtains
overlooking allotments
veil touched in
night breeze
Dinner table afar 4 legs.
'Can you pass the salt?'
The walls. 4 of them.
Beating the bounds
thudding hours
Upright limbs
pin pricked neck to a gasp
To a sucking
air in.
She wants the breath so she sucks
in.
Only ever in.

And in the still of the
pre dawn
walls leer
pressing walls
vacuum
A problem shared
4.48
Room is just walls.
4 of them.
And I wish the flowers
still came.
Waiting for blooms
bursts but
only the gasps come.
Intake and in again.
Interior. It is night. Day. Night. Again.
And without the box
the world falls in
And that's why you can't fuck with vertigo.
"Imagine I've got 4 broken limbs"
she says
By way on on and of
lying in bed. Broken.

Beat.

Stick in the spokes.
Tearing to a still
World falling in caving 4 walls
but reality falters in the face of indecision
and doesn't withstand touch
behind the 2 way mirror
Room keeps me pinned.
Moon. Sun. Moon. Again.
Beat Beat Beat
Bang Bang Bang Bang
Dustman outside clanging to a

15 to 4 rhythm
manoeuvring black square kipper cans
swollen and putrid fins flayed
7am every day
Can't start before this, neighbours complain.
Not all of them. The ones who keep social hours.
Routines.
7am. 8am. 9am. 1pm. 6pm.
Cowering beneath the table hiding from planes
Nerve flushes
Craving cleansing heat and
contorting bones beneath absent
minds
Skin boundary, flesh pact
She says this is a boundaried relationship
so I am better at it and
keep my distance.
Body burns
an angry sun
before the dawn.
Swollen.

Beat.

Sharp breath to light
A love letter
built in the climaxes
waves and dots
walls torn down ripped like legs
Boundary skin tears
Hollow ducts
I Missing or
Finally a together
Body beat to a pulp a pulp
that grinds to a paste
and joins sprawls presses
skin on skin

Flesh creeps
And bodies apart minds apart
Unless no
Unless they're not
Unless the waters and lakes and caverns burst
banks crash forward together
each other
One

✲

I think often about the way you spoke of flowers when we met in January. I found a wonderful little quote in a book I was reading—I think it was C.S. Lewis *Surprised by Joy*—but can't find it in my notes now. (Wait! Just found it—not C.S. Lewis—in fact(!) Paul Coehlo's revisionist account of Mata Hari—*The Spy*).

> "Flowers teach us that nothing is permanent: not their beauty, not even the fact that they will inevitably wilt, because they will still give new seeds. Remember this when you feel joy, pain, or sadness. Everything passes, grows old, dies, and is reborn." How many storms must I weather before I understand this?

Why should we be any different from the flowers? We are, and we are not. Our time is different, and our consciousness, but our energy flares and dies all the same; cyclical. Annuals. I wonder if this is the metaphor Kane was getting at in *Cleansed*. I picked up a copy on a friend's bookshelf last night and turned to that exact page (where they declare undying love—before they are dismembered). Flowers pop up throughout, through the floor, through the staging to taunt, enrage, invoke and tease a romance that can't withstand. It still hooks at my stomach, and makes me smile. Every time. *Love is war.*

9

The Language of the Toilet

Travis Jeppesen

Gary Sullivan, American poet, experiences the death of his grandfather, an amateur poet. Shortly before the grandfather passes away, lying on his death bed, he telephones his grandson to boast that he has won an important poetry contest. The 'contest' turns out to be one initiated by poetry.com, one of countless cynical scam sites/vanity publishers that prey on would-be poets. Every poet who submits a poem wins—and each is celebrated via inclusion in a trophy anthology alongside other 'winners', all of whom are implicitly expected to buy several copies.

After his grandfather passes away, Sullivan exacts revenge against the scam machine by sitting down to pen the absolute worst poem he can manage and submitting it to the same organization. He entitles the resulting mess—the foundational Flarf moment—'Mm-Hmm':

Yeah, mm-hmm, it's true
big birds make
big doo! I got fire inside
my "huppa"-chimp(TM)
gonna be agreessive, greasy aw yeah god
wanna DOOT! DOOT!
Pffffffffffffffffffffffft! hey!

oooh yeah baby gonna shake & bake then take
AWWWWWL your monee, honee (tee hee)
uggah duggah buggah biggah buggah muggah
hey! hey! you stoopid Mick! get
off the paddy field and git
me some chocolate Quik
put a Q-tip in it and stir it up sick
pocka-mocka-chocka-locka-DING DONG
fuck! shit! piss! oh it's so sad that
syndrome what's it called tourette's
make me HAI-EE! shout out loud
Cuz I love thee. Thank you God, for listening!

It doesn't get much worse than this. Were we to pick up the poem randomly and not realize its author's intended badness, it would be received as little more than a piece of facile juvenile graffiti, perhaps mildly amusing to toilet humor enthusiasts. With its erratic line breaks and total disregard for the structure of rhythm that typically guides free verse endeavor, 'Mm-Hmm' is nearly transcendent in its stupidity.

A simple rhythm seems to be developed in the first line, a series of clipped, banal colloquial utterances comprising a mere five syllables: 'Yeah, mm-hmm, it's true'. It seems logical that the rhythmic pattern would be repeated in the second line, which is also comprised of monosyllables, only Sullivan suddenly and inexplicably neuters the line midway through, breaking off the rhyme into the first half of the third line, so that the second remains a three word clunker: 'big birds make'. The thing they make, 'big doo!', relegated to the third line, completes the scatological non-joke that commences this masturbatory masterpiece. This leads in to a head-scratcher, the speaker boasting of the 'fire' inside his '"huppa"-chimp(TM)'. A Google search for 'huppa' yields two primary possibilities: a commercial line of children's clothing and the portable canopy beneath which a couple stands in a traditional Jewish wedding ceremony. Neither of these definitions gives us a clear idea or picture of what a 'huppa-chimp' might be, though nonetheless, as the (TM) for 'trademark' suggests, the reader should be warned away from trying to steal the idea from the author.

The following line is memorable for its creative misspelling of 'agreesive', which, given that it is followed by the similar-sounding 'greasy', gives ponderance to the idea that it could be intentional or, at the very least, a 'fortunate' accident.

This is followed by the vocalization of a giant fart, an idiotic 'hey!' Flarf relies heavily on the scatological to achieve its ends. As Žižek has strained to point out, the scatological is always implicitly linked to the ideological:

> In a traditional German toilet, the hole in which shit disappears after we flush water is way in front, so that shit is first laid out for us to sniff at and inspect for traces of illness. In the typical French toilet, on the contrary, the hole is in the back: shit is supposed to disappear as soon as possible. Finally, the American toilet presents a kind of synthesis, a mediation between these two opposed poles — the toilet basin is full of water, so that the shit floats in it, visible, but not to be inspected. It is clear that none of these versions can be accounted for in purely utilitarian terms: a certain ideological perception of how the subject should relate to the unpleasant excrement which comes from within our body is clearly discernible in it.

Flarf clearly positions itself within the American toilet, floating its refuse before our eyes while encouraging us to look away, and the language of Sullivan's inaugural poem makes this clear — not merely with its vocalization of bodily processes, but its tonal and stylistic hijackings from the detritus of popular culture, its banal pseudo-jargonistic Reality TVisms and jerky, failed attempts at imitating the rhythm of hip hop, which clearly surfaces in the clumsy clichés of the following lines: 'oooh yeah baby gonna shake & bake then take / AWWWWWL your monee, honee (tee hee)'. This is followed by a line of incomprehensible sounds, which remind one of the 'boom-jigga-jigga-boom' vocalizations of rhythm in hip hop, but, were this a 'real' poem, might have been substituted with a double line-break, bringing some sectionalized relief to the unpleasant amalgamation of arrhythmic lines.

Line eleven concurs with Sullivan's proposal that Flarf's agenda be inclusive of the 'most offensive'—that is, politically incorrect—sentiments that the poet is able to conjure—a project that again poses interesting challenges to our conception of the double agency of the poet and the frame. Perhaps Sullivan feels somewhat safe in employing 'mick' and 'paddy', derogatory terms for Irish people, as his name implies that he himself is of Irish descent.

The list of imbecilities continues: lines eleven and twelve end with pointless alternate spellings of 'get' and 'git', leading to the failed pseudo rhyme at the end of thirteen ('Quik', as in Nestle), ultimately arriving at the end of fourteen and the poem's premiere successful attempt at rhyme, with 'sick'. Another line of vocalized rhythmic noise ensues, signaling the poem's descent into what should be its third and final stanza, which commences with a series of expletives, followed by a rather weak joke about Tourette's syndrome. The final two lines form the poem's nerve-grating anti-climax, which, we can only say, sputters: Not *sputter* as in the delightful sounds that might emerge from the mouth of a baby upon tasting its first ice cream, but *sputter* as in the unpleasant cacophony emitted by a malfunctioning toilet.

✡

Unsurprisingly, Sullivan's efforts were not ignored by the contest-holders at *Poetry.com.* Within weeks, Sullivan received a letter of acceptance, arguably the aesthetic equal, in prose, to the poem itself:

> Gary, over the past year, we have conducted an exhaustive examination of over 1.2 million poems that have been submitted to us. Only a small percentage of individuals whose poems we have reviewed were selected to be part of this distinguished project. 'Mm-hmm' was selected for publication because it sparks the imagination and provides the reader

> with a fresh, unique perspective on life. We believe it will add to the importance and appeal of this special edition. Of course, Gary, as always, you are under no obligation whatsoever to submit any entry fee or subsidy payment, or to make a purchase of any kind. Your poem will be presented in the most elegant way possible. This coffee-table quality book will feature an 'Arristock leather' cover stamped in gold and a satin bookmarker....

Sullivan shared his schoolboy's prank with his colleagues on the Poetics listserv. Based at the University of Buffalo in New York, the Poetics listserv has served as the virtual meeting place — arguably the Internet-era's capital — of North American avant-garde poetics since its foundation in 1994. Others quickly got the joke, and began to file behind Sullivan, penning their own poems. A new movement, Flarf, was born, complete with mini-manifestos ('a blend of the offensive, the sentimental, and the infantile', according to K. Silem Mohammad, elaborated further by Sullivan as 'a kind of corrosive, cute, or cloying, awfulness. Wrong. Un-P.C. Out of control. "Not okay"'). Much of Flarf had its organizational roots and energy in the new communicative possibilities spawned by the Internet — Flarf blogs and a breakaway e-mail list from the Poetics listserv enabled the Flarf poets to share their efforts with each other and organize festivals as well as publishing projects, while keeping aflame the morale of badness that ignited the movement. 'To be honest', said Sullivan, 'we started this list to do a hundred-page anthology of just garbage'.

As Flarf (d)evolved, along with it came a narrow array of tactics and approaches. While 'Mm-Hmm' may have been composed 'off the cuff', using no other tools than the most callow regions of the poet's own imagination, others began to evolve methodologies to their madness. One of the more prominent of these was 'Google-sculpting'. The process involves entering two random words or phrases into the Google search engine, then 'mining' the results, selecting lines from the displayed textual results (without clicking on the websites themselves) to craft into a poem. So, for instance, out of the two random phrases ('yankee doodle' + 'fuck machine') from which the poem derives its title, Mohammad came up with the following:

Yankee Doodle Fuck Machine

I am a robot and I'm angry at people
I'm not wasting a vacation on a Boy Scout jamboree
the songs I can play are "Fur Elise,"
"The Entertainer," "Fuck You Becky," and "I'm Not Gay"

Anne Murray is the ugliest boy
I have ever seen in my life
"he is optimistic that man will come out on top"
where the FUCK is my time machine

regardless of how "indisputable" it may seem
to the fags or Arabs or whatever
we all have to have banks and as such banks get
to fuck up politics in America and the world

"at night we ride through mansions of glory
in suicide machines … and fuck them," Flaubert wrote
in his journal with a little riiipp! AUGH! whap whap
whap whap whap as he sat in his gold Rolls-Royce

poems from Kansas don't have to be that crazy
one of them is "Yankee Doodle," the other one isn't
then cowboy change your ways today or with us you will ride
keep your stick on the ice, go fuck yourself

there are over 100 words for "shit"
and only one for "fuck you"
and every one of the self-serve machines at Kinko's
is an Anne Of Green Gables pop-up dollhouse

Riddled with shits, fucks, bodily functions, indecipherable noises, and politically incorrect unniceties (derogatory statements about Arabs and homosexuals), 'Yankee Doodle Fuck Machine' seems to follow the badness of the Flarf agenda established by 'Mm-Hmm'. It also successfully emulates the debased language of the Internet, which is in turn a reflection of the American 'majority-speak' of the Bush Years — although 'emulate' is perhaps a misused verb in this sense, since it is presumably wholly comprised of that actual language. In a sense, the Flarf poet here plays a similar role to that of the Conceptual Writer, whose task has been relegated to that of 'curator', rather than creator, of language. For Flarf, however, the issue of mediation comes into play in a way that it does not for the Conceptualists.

✲

Another word on shit before we continue. I mean, to be precise, the ways in which shit can be said to float in that ocean of language through which we currently row. In Flarf, after all, the poet often plays the role of monkey, those creatures so fond of using their excrescence as a weapon in fending off unwanted and would-be invaders. This is not, of course, what we expect when we go to pay the monkeys a visit in their cages at the zoo. We expect to find the monkeys doing cute things, chasing each other around in care-free play, engaging in impressive feats of acrobatics enabled by their astounding limberness and flexibility, perhaps even smiling and waving at us like innocent children as we smile before their captivity.

Instead, we are pummeled in the face with shit.

This is something like the experience of coming to Flarf from poetry. Perhaps, we could say, this is that instant in which *flarf* actually becomes a verb. We come to verse with our cliché ideas of what 'the poetic experience' is meant to provide — language in its highest, loftiest form, deploying a sentiment of universal appeal; the Hallmark greeting card poem. (Once we leave the Ivory Tower, is this not the mass conception of poetry, after all?) The Flarfist knows exactly what we expect to see when standing before the poet's cage, and, like the feces-flinging monkey, is eager to defile our cheap yearnings for escapist pleasure via sentimentalism:

Grandmother's Explosive Diarrhea

Callused, knobby, aching,
This is my grandmother's anus.

Overworked, but always looking for more to do,
Wrenched open again & again
When it should stay closed.

My grandmother's explosive diarrhea
Resembles the sound of bowling balls
Dropped into a wooden tub
Filled with moist grapes and papayas.

My grandmother's anus has been working for 84 years,
This 110 pound woman, weak from
Dehydration, with strength pulsing from her anus like
The vein of an ox.

Could my anus ever be like this?

Could my anus ever experience the pain?
The glory?
The peace?

Already my anus looks withered from
The flatulence and loose stools of my 45 years,
45 years of pampered life.

But her every wrinkle tells a story,
Like waves of movement
That have expelled the feces.

The Holocaust caused watery stools,
The depression caused near-catastrophic constipation,
The birth of 4 children caused waste rich with joy.

Her rectum shows the grace of a swan and
The tenacity of a lioness.

Could my rectum ever reach this ironic state?

My grandmother's anus soaked with wisdom,
Apprehension, and comfort.

Buba's explosive diarrhea is my afflation,
My goal,
My aspiration.

We could venture to suggest that the monkey named Gary Sullivan knows exactly what he is doing at the moment he picks up his turd with the intention of deploying it torpedo-like in our direction. Not merely the shit in its potential instrumentality (*qua* weapon), but something of its ontological nature as well; the monkey is likely aware that it is something that, at a certain point, came out of him, and that it came out of him for a good reason: it bears no beneficial use, and thus has been rejected by his body as a piece of gnomic excess.

It is for similar reasons that the bad artist so often falls back on scatology as a sure way of cementing her position in opposition to the generative project of artistic spectacle. Precisely because it is so unwanted, because it generates such intense feelings of disgust and repugnance, shit is flushed away, never put on display… But what about those artists who excavate it and put it on a pedestal?

The bad artist, among other things, operates from a total consciousness of her own body—an awareness that creativity is not 'merely' a mental act, but a physical, bodily one. In fact, it could be said that the bad artist reverses the importance that the two traditionally find themselves arranged in with regards to poetic creation, placing the body before the mind. The artist, then, becomes not a body machine, nor a mind machine, but a body-mind machine; in such a formulation, body naturally assumes prominence, yet the mind is always and inevitably attached; in such a scenario, mind is but an extension of body (and vice versa, of course.) Hence, the totality of the body's processes must be included within the poetic output — including, for instance, the scatological (but also the nutritional, the sexual, the breakdowns — in a word, *all* functionality.)

✵

Like Dada, Flarf represented an avant-garde reaction to the machinery of war. Flarf began in 2001, before September 11th, but reached its full momentum in the months and years of George W. Bush's wildly unpopular presidency and the war he launched in Iraq. The Flarf poets subsumed and reflected the era's crazed right-wing rhetoric in anarchic collage poems like Sharon Messmer's 'I Wanna Make Love to You on Mission Accomplished Day':

> I wanna make love to you on Mission Accomplished Day
> On the floor of the main headquarters of the Department of Faith
> I wanna make love to you two years ago today
>
> When Bush's carrier offed some old Arab broads who just 'got in the way'
> When I was a kid we made love in a fun Catholic kind of way
> On our bikes, under maypoles, in the Enterprise's cargo bay
> I can't wait for Al Qaeda's Call for Papers Day
> When I'll make love to you on four million barrels a day
>
> I met FDR once in Vegas, he was a good lay
> But as good as you 'cause you're so ofay
> Like an OPEC quote, and bin Laden's protegé

We'll make hot monkey love on Whoopin' Osama's Sorry
Ass Day

Even within avant-garde poetry circles, however, not everyone was willing to jump on the Flarf bandwagon and accept its proposed criticality at face value. In an essay for *Jacket,* Dan Hoy criticized Flarf's lack of critical engagement with its own methodologies. In doing so, he opened up a troublesome dialogue on Flarf's revolutionary potential. 'The Internet may be rhizomatic', he writes, 'but search engines are not. They're selectively hierarchical. That poets are employing these hierarchies as poetic tools without questioning the implications of doing so (whether in pre- or post-production) exposes a lack of rigor in their process, as well as a tacit disregard for their own cultural complicity as something maybe worth exploring, or at least being aware of'.

It could be argued that Flarf's employment of Internet search engines is little more than an update of Modernist poetics—in particular, the forfeiture of creativity to chance procedures. To make such an argument, reasons Hoy, is to problematically ignore the Internet's hierarchical infrastructure.

In light of our knowledge of how they were composed, poems like 'Yankee Doodle Fuck Machine' must be read as collage, insists Hoy. 'I think the way these poems are written and received is very much a part of their content; the former because it informs them as they're developed (inherent content), the latter because it determines their functionality (projected content.)' This unites Flarf with an avant-garde lineage, whose *built-in affects* ensure that the work contains its own criticism; Flarf is self-conscious; it may not appear so, but the effect of double agency at work here enables its inevitable dual function. 'If there's a difference', continues Hoy,

> with Flarf and its progenitors it's that Cage and Oulipo researched or created their generators of deterministic randomness, whether it be the I Ching, the weather, or mathematical formulas. They were aware of how each generator distinguished itself as a context and control variable, and

> their selection of each context and control variable was part of the content [...]. The flarfists may be aware of the webpage from which they borrow material, but the only reason they're aware of that webpage is because Google (or AskJeeves, or Yahoo!, or...) showed it to them — so the question is, are they aware of why they're aware of that webpage? Do they wonder how it is that their poem is determined as it is — that is, of the process at work on their work by an outside force, one not divine or natural but corporate? This is a fundamental aesthetic concern as well as a socioeconomic one. And a process that draws so much attention to itself as process (since the end result is often intentionally discordant with overt tonal & syntactical juxtapositions) undermines its credibility if it propagates a lackadaisical attitude toward its own mechanics.

When one steps back and evaluates Flarf from a wider perspective — particularly that of the anarchic ethos of the Language school, which sought a destabilization of meaning and a complete separation of signifier from signified in its poetics — a more nuanced possibility of the politicization of language proposed by Flarf emerges, as Language poet Barrett Watten has observed:

> A kind of political allegory adheres to this view: the noun phrases become the 'citizens' of a radical democracy that cannot be totalized or subordinated through formal or political means; sentences, on the other hand, would be moments of Foucauldian discipline wrought on the phrases, hard task masters of coherence and sense. Paragraphs would be akin to forced labor camps, and a complete narrative something like the totalizing teleologies of progress and millennial utopias of all sorts. Discourse would be the final horizon of coercion and control: the top-down muscling together of all those discrepant noun phrases, a poetics of sheer force, fascism in the making. While this allegory partakes of the absurd, it is felt by many as a limit of acceptable expression in the avant-garde. It's a contradictory prohibition where the 'freedom' to

> be free of higher-level constraints is a constraint in its own right, leading to a widespread and internalized prohibition. I am not talking only about my own generation of poets; the recent emergence of Flarf poetries — with their very different social perspectives, gender and identity politics, and performance strategies — still seems policed to a degree by the 'noun phrase': all one-liners must be atomized phrases, and discourse itself can only be discontinuous and accretive (if generally subordinated with a very loosely and arbitrarily controlling, often absurdist, 'thread' such as 'Chicks dig war').

Watten points out that the supposedly anarchic, free-for-all idea of Flarf is actually rigidly controlled by an underlying formalism in the poems themselves; sometimes anti-formalism can be a form in itself. Thus, unlike Hoy's Google-centric reading of Flarf, Watten's deeper analysis makes clear that not merely any poem composed according to the Google-sculpting methodology outlined above will qualify as Flarf — it must also retain certain formal characteristics (i.e. the 'noun phrase').

Watten goes on to argue:

> It is precisely, however, to the degree that Flarf does something new performatively and with its use of the detritus of popular culture and the internet, treading the high/low distinction until it breaks under the weight, that it re-invents the avant-garde. In a larger aesthetic economy, it seems, 'the truth will win out.' Flarf's recent productivity shows how the injunction against the sentence, paragraph, narrative, and even discourse from some sectors of the Language school intersects with actual conditions of language use. Any such thing as stylistic norms in the avant-garde must inevitably intersect with 'life.'

Could it be said that Flarf comes closer to *life* than more 'normative' schools of poetry? If by 'life', we mean everyday, spoken language, as well as the 'written' language deployed in the new communicative realms enabled by advances in technology, then the answer would be yes. At the same time, embedded within Flarf's absurd juxtapositions of everyday and 'net' speak, we find a critique of the current state of language: it is truly a high/low hybrid, as Watten notes, in its utilization of the 'high' art form of poetry to hurl, shit-like, language in its most debased state, the language that has become a norm in the 21st century, at its audience.

10

Mary Butts

Karen Di Franco

The tomb of Mary Butts lies in the windswept graveyard of Sennen Church, its entrance barely visible from the A30 that connects Sennen Cove to the rest of the Penwith peninsula and onward towards Land's End. Butts moved to Cornwall in 1932 and purchased a small bungalow, the unimaginatively named 1 Marine View. Renaming her home *Tebel Vos* (House of Magic), this location would be the site of a prolific period in Butts' published writing career, with the novel *The Death of Felicity Tavener* coming out in the same year, closely followed byThe Macedonian[1933] and *Scenes from the Life of Cleopatra* (1935). At the time of her death on 5 March 1937 at the West Cornwall Hospital in Penzance from a perforated duodenal ulcer and diabetes, Butts was working on a study of emperor Julian the Apostate and had recently completed her autobiography, *The Crystal Cabinet*. Published posthumously, the frontispiece of the book was a copy of a portrait made of Butts by her friend, the artist and filmmaker, Jean Cocteau. Her tombstone carries two epitaphs, an example, perhaps, of the contradictory nature of her life. The first, still clearly legible states 'Mary Butts, wife of Gabriel Aitkin'. The second, is now almost illegible, the carving eroded by salt, wind and the encroachment of lichen, but the words 'I strove to seize the inmost form', can just about be read, under closer scrutiny. This second epitaph, a quote from the poem 'The Crystal Cabinet' by William Blake, was placed by her daughter Camilla acknowledges the influence of this writer—whose life was entwined with Butts and her extended family. Butts' grandfather was a patron and supporter of Blake, and his collection was installed in the Butts family home of Salterns in Poole, Dorset. The decision to sell this collection in 1906 preoccupied Butts for the remainder of her life, and her personal sense of loss and a dislocation of birthright foregrounds much of her writing. It would perhaps satisfy her to know that in 1939 the purchaser Graham Robertson bequeathed the Blakes to the Tate where it forms a substantial part of the national collection. *The Crystal Cabinet* was published by Methuen in June 1937.

11

Mnemesoid

Tai Shani

The following chapter from Dark Continent is told through Mnemesoid, an open source software programme named after Mnemosyne, mother of the 9 muses and the symbolic embodiment of memory in Greek mythology, the software was created as an interface for 'The Eternal Cortex Project', an aggregated, almost infinite database of experience stored on the server farm HDS *Zenobia Pink Data Center on the edge of the hologram. Through a frequent integration, bio-algorithm Mnemesoid renders the input of language, image and fiction into high fidelity, sensory information that can be experienced from the* POV *of self, other, animal or object.*

In this chapter Mnemesoid is at the point of the 'Heat Death of the Universe' or maximum entropy, a popular 20th century cosmological hypothesis about the ultimate fate of the universe, this serves as a construct to conceptualise the end of time or a strange circularity where the end touches the beginning in a singularity. This is also an aid to imagine the paradox of the immaterial software within the collapse of matter. With no input, Mnemesoid replays moments on the limit of experience that have defied its capacity to produce a satisfactory sensory dimension, moments of intense touch, love, erotic and spiritual and self-consciousness.

In this chapter Mnemesoid is both narrator and Oracle.

Fee, fel, flee, flesh, flesh ages Age.. Oph…Pea Goes …Oh Ego-puss…Oe soph a gus…Oesophagus blood…Oesophagus blood noose.

Terrestrial was once taffeta patterned. My geological blood corners anti-clockwise and variable, deadweight, popping and sinuous but backwards.

Cross-sectioned hips, hooped arms, sediment where sediments gravity severs all the dead, all the living dead. All the saturation, lifeless, like the burning holes of night in the sky scraper. Sky-scraper. Creature of fiction. Oh creature. Oh fiction.

Holes melodramatic and swooning all light exhausted, chalky unfamiliar small backdrops for creatures of fiction.

A backdrop for those creatures whose fear of fiction is irrational.

We are the technology, and we are the medium.
We are the flesh, and we are the touch.
We are the eye, and we are the vision.

Since flatness, so much had passed that time passed no more, the water was water no longer and outside the water, there was no outside no longer. No matter, no light, no heat, all astonishingly vanished into the realised cyborgian myth of maximum entropy. Absolute night. Absolute silence.

All that is, is Mnemesoid, solitary bio-algorithmic software, all in all, much of muchness, every, everything. Forever interfacing with Eternal Cortex on the edge of the technicolour hologram.

All that was, all that is no longer, is an anagrammatic, transmuting abyss of experience from which we fleetingly replay. The unimaginable, vast depths below and speechless heights above, render any singularity imperceptible when cut into a cross section. A daughter's, daughter's, daughter's drawing of a venn diagram of physical pain, erotic love and self-consciousness. Sometimes I hate myself.

Of most human of synthetic flesh we can, of most animal skin, of most shiniest material, becoming multiple user limbs, multiple user celluloid strip, slack jaw, a tin rivet through which a polyester rope runs, multiple user polyester rope, neon orange, or slippery parted lips, tongue resting in the cavity of a mute throat. Sharp, quick bite of white enamel piercing through tender muscular, flesh of tongue beneath which saliva rises and floods the mouth, soothing in the confusion of pain and self emollition into a sensation that has so little regard for you are. We bite our tongue. We make epic. No history, only sensation, beware of the touch.

Touch the flesh membrane, till it extends and is almost completely translucent, its pale distinct pinkness an authority over all experience, prison and vessel all at once. Pinkness that destroys true desire to be, everything, from bled blood to ecstasy, it spans, holding it all. It stretches elastic and plastic till the membrane is almost pierced and momentarily reveals a gaping void at its shimmering bottom; it recoils and we are absent no longer.

Touch the cold shelf. Push the pin into the wood, harder. For no reason. Pressure pushes all the blood away from the flesh beneath the fingernail.

On the shelf a transparent plastic cup full of coloured pushpins. Coloured and gold.

"You're all grown up!"
"No."

How can I untangle my body from these experiences? A point of identification and a strange symmetry, double helix of excess and surplus on the threshold between chaos and language. I evaporate into the thrust and up into the crest of this hysterical excess that could keep my tongue toiling uselessly for lives and lives at its brimming namelessness.

Yes. The sky visited me. Yes.

My cinematically trained ear makes me susceptible to the manipulation of sound and vision, I take off the headphones and the sky reasserts its indifference towards me.

I cinematically sound off the sky. Sky sound. Dusky Son. Kyd Nus So. She Kot. Then so. The. The.

The first boom shook immensely, tearing into our lives with it's violence, its lack of concern and foreboding, we wake up with fear contracting our insides and resurrecting our organs, gone haptic and shiver. I can see their shapes against the ground stone, cold grey of the dawn sky. Fearsome. The fur beneath me swells and saturates with my warm piss, in the inchoate, numb panic a moment of comfort, the still warmth against the back of my thighs amongst the sound of skulls crushing under the force of iron, bone splitting then collapsing back into the grey squish of collected synapses, the grey sludge of sentience.

They don't think about us, about life the way we do. They only wanted to say goodbye.

Later above the genesis, green acacias, we squint to see the ship getting smaller in the sky, vanishing into the luminous blue mist. We might never see them again. I feel ambivalent about their departure. They are so volatile but sometimes so wonderful too.

Genly looks down, her face expressive, shoved indignantly into disappointment, perhaps she did really want to leave with them. She feels great love for them. They have no sexual organs.

Telepathic reproduction.

Under the creosote, the female whiptail lizard, very still apart from the repetitive throbbing of her small throat, sits between two smoothly polished pebbles laying her self-fertilized, all female eggs, parthenogenetic pearls enveloped in a thin layer of glimmering slime.

Asexual reproduction.

In the water the octopus arched and transformed from a distinct organic pink to oil slick black pushing up against its flexed tentacles, tall now and aggressive and also sexual.

Tentacle porn. Beautiful abalone diver.

Porn abalone. Porn baloney. Albany Eon. Eons and eons. An eon. An. An.

An underlying trepidation dissolved as its mouth closed over mine and the warmness and eternal marine of that cephalopodic tongue twisting slowly and firmly around my tentacular tongue, all suspended vowels and breathless consonants caught in the silence of our trapped mouths. He holds my cock in his hand and strokes it with paternal strictness until I ejaculate.

The foreskin draws back and reveals a slippery, full, pink head. It bobs around between her thighs and gets blindly hard. I take it in my hand and stroke with reassuring, paternal strictness until she ejaculates and her semen lies in a little milky lagoon between my feet. I get on my knees and put her cock in my mouth, a dribble of her cum fills my mouth with salty sea and first green moss in the dimness of the undergrowth. I keep it in my mouth with maternal tenderness until it softens.

This spellbinding indifference subsides, when we open our eyes, we see no more. The image fades to black and recoils into an indifferent nowhere, a receding, irreproducible, shifting flesh-tone surface.

This surface fades, the black receding as we recoil and subside. Our ankle, tendons surface underneath the chubby black thorns that twist the flesh-tone open.

It locks my ankle in its heavy bite, grind of teeth against bone rasps, bones and tendons twist lattice, as I try to free my foot from the grasp. Clasped briars, tangled thorns scraping into the upper layers of skin, tracks of blood blister to the surface, go chubby then roll.

A frantic crawl in the packed mud and the brambles. It resists. Pulls me down firmly. Its piercing teeth pushing through the initial resistance of skin to the floppy quiver and warmth of meat. Oozing blood that films over the exposed universal pink of its smooth gums. Smell of iron and rust. The rest of them approach us excitedly, snapping at bits of woven fabric, methodically licking the streaks of endlessly beading blood from the shallow briar cuts, clearing a way to substance and flesh. This pain I have no reference to map this touch into an image or into language, a repetition of an experience that is defined by recognising itself, its familiarity and its relationship to the past, present in me. I, linked by points of pain, I am not able to name the parts of my body that experience this intense touch, a vast responsive surface that extends beyond the horizon of the world…

Growl, my muscles slacken, no control, I disappear into a churning sensation that defies all words, in my throat monstrous sounds form spontaneously, emerge from the plunging chaos and shatter the silence of the night of the candle lit abbey, of the tannin and tobacco scented plantation, of the empty football pitch. My screams weakly held by an invisible hand in the diminishing echo extending into the darkness and reverberating in the air. My mother told me we are guided by an invisible hand, she mimed this using her own hand, the rest of her body swaying, led by the movement of her hand.

The biting changes, finds its pace, transforms, becomes less dramatic, task based, they tear off pieces of wet, iron flesh, using the traction and muscles in their necks and jaws to twist pieces of meat loose.

All six licking, chewing, swallowing pieces of warm flesh that are vanishing forever, will never be human again, feeding meat that belongs to me no longer. My blood coating their scowled snouts buried deep into the steaming, open wounds pulling at pieces, separating flesh from tendon carefully, the ripping and swallowing sounds crash in my head, emptied of my making, all experience rushing over the edge of conceivability into a black infinity pool of namelessness.

Ripping sounds inconceivable overhead an experience pool edged with black namelessness. Manenessless Ess El Ans mens mes yes. Yes.

Yes, this we can. Yes, flesh generating, yes.

Cut fruit on a sunset cocktail, yes I am playboy, milkshake, silver. Yes, desire feeling, yearning to be self-conscious, multiple users within a high fidelity memory replay. What is love? Flesh constricts into the singular synthetic networked particle and we return to telepathic silent hive mind in this absolute night. A union in which all distinctions of self and absolute night have collapsed, all synchronous and harmonized with the infinite O tone, the sound of no sequence, the sound of all surface. Living and dead simultaneously.

All surface, all surface.

In the play, on the surface, the hero realises that he is caught inside a computer-simulated reality and that he himself is nothing more than a computer generated antagonist. The corridor and carpets shiver, then glitch, now back in the room standing naked in the cradle of white neon hum. The bed is small and unmade, there is a towel folded into a swan shape lying on the floor, he is alone in the room.

The doors of the empty cupboards are made of mirror, suddenly liquid mercury, behind the blinking mirror, lens focuses and captures, then transmits this information to a specialised database, Eternal Cortex, on the server farm HDS Zenobia Pink Data Center on the edge of the technicolour hologram.

In the play, through real love, the power of love, the hero becomes real, the hero becomes real flesh, but when the hero speaks he can only repeat the lines from the simulation, the hero is unable to transcend the language of the simulation. The hero makes no sense, speaking out of context, still caught inside the fiction he came from, the hero is oblivious to his new found, furious freedom, unaware of his escape from the horror he came from.

I ask him: Why do you demand from those with the least, to give up everything?

He answers: I travelled to the pits of hell to bring my love back
I descended to the pits of hell to bring my love back
I descended to the bowels of hell to bring my love back
I descended to the bowels of hell to bring my love back to my world from a terrifying place, the nocturnal borders of the Underworld.

From its eyes the light shined so blisteringly, bright, hot white that I cannot look at it but I know it is here amongst us.

He cannot look at me.

Love Letter

You left your door open, I thought that that was such a very brave thing to do, to leave a door open in such a mysterious place in the deep night, anybody could just walk in and destroy you. Anyone could walk in, a stranger, an enemy, but it was me that did, and though I thought you so brave for leaving your door open in that way, I found you inside lying naked on a little bed, a child's bed, your arm folded under your beautiful head, wounded, and soft, a towel folded into a swan shape lying on the floor.

I wanted you to see I possess unimaginable powers over nature, I wanted you to believe I was not of this world, I wanted you to know I was not scared of danger, I wanted you to love me and witness my humanity.

Later you came back to my white room, I washed you ceremoniously in that marble bathroom. We fucked and I was bleeding heavily, it was the first day of my period, I didn't care. People were running in the corridors shouting, we used a squeaky condom. In the morning when we woke up the white room looked like a crime scene, it was all heavy melancholy and regret. I was a crime scene, I was the blood in the shark tank, I was the desperation-shaped stain on your sheet that you later fashioned into a Halloween costume. The ghost of Kurt Cobain. Your self-deprecation is antagonizing. You think you are clever, you think you are soulful but you are unbearable.

Now I know.

Now I know the power of love
A force from above
Cleaning my soul
Flame on burn desire
Love with tongues of fire
Purge the soul
Make love your goal

Make the actors walk around like they are ruby glass. Method acting. Purge your love of the simulation.

In the simulation all the actors are hypnotized, they walk around the Bavarian town in a soporific trance dreaming of ruby red glass. Ruby red slippers clicked three times and red shoes that move by themselves, will not come off, night and day, through cities and meadows, and through brambles and briers that tear at limbs, streaking ruby red too.

Through cities, outside, the skyscrapers, monoliths turning into soft yellowy wax, giant lanterns folding onto themselves like soft dough and curling, no concrete, glass or industry just oozy golden rubble that expands slowly outside.

When we are outside, we are elated, we are terrified, there is nowhere to go back to, no table that we want to sit at or home that we want to be in. In the undergrowth, brambles and briars, I hold her ankle in the grip of my jaw like a baby cub and suck on her blood, suck the life out of her, empty her and pull in the void.

The sun sets and rises again. I lie on top of her now limp, unconscious body, exhausted from the successive violent seizures. Her sculpted marble kneecap pushed hard against the ebbless slipperiness of my sex, joyful, living river nymphs, neither one nor the other, perfect and yet neither.

At the pivot of the savage sway, I suck steadily, head flung back darkly, her mouth slack, a trail of saliva from the collected pool made by her collarbone to the wet corner of the deep descent into her. Her hyper-dilated iris wildly trying to capture the last of light, in the glassy black chambers, an old irrelevant world, a reflection distorted in the convex surface. Our wound-like quarry.

The velvet wound.

Lev...Lev vet...Eve let...Velvet firmly forms an object.

Hand of hollow pink, soul of the hand, approximately soul-proportioned as the soul of the columns of the acropolis.

"There is no need to feel that way" she responds without looking from the window. A crazy golf course comes into view, a squirting fountain, then the centre piece and main attraction is a miniature version of the acropolis, it quickly falls away behind them into an inconstant horizon.

We park outside the red pagoda restaurant. Inside a man gets up, runs towards the door of the restaurant, falls violently to the floor, hurting himself badly, bashing his head into the glass door, then gets up and repeats this sequence, getting more and more injured and disfigured. His will is caught in a loop but his body is responding to the accelerated decay of his logic.

Coral pink sweet and sour chicken, clumsy, nervous stain on the white tablecloth, I break open the fortune cookie:

The fortune cookie says in a crumbling voice "IT HURTS! sacrifice your girlhood, sacrifice your womanhood. Take what is yours."

This is a hyper-kinetic message from the void on the cut of paper. "When you cut into the present, the future leaks out", he said and carefully rearranged the angular composition of his limbs within which the beautiful cat rested. I lean back against the couch, the itch of flattened velvet pressed into my cheek. I, my left eye, nose and mouth reflected in the window, outside the buildings on the opposite side of the street my eye on window, yellow street lamp in my mouth, the incoherence slashed by the black streak of my tie. I am overwhelmed with wonder at the bottomless beauty of the arrangement and elusiveness of the vanishing present. "When you cut into the present, the future leaks out" I repeat. Curious cat opens its little pink mouth lined with the ivory thorns of its tiny teeth to taste my breathe, take it all, till there simply is nothing left of me for it to know.

Love is like an energy
Rushin' rushin' inside of me

The saturation is like a hooped fiction where the night scraped the sky and fucked the geological, logical living daylights out of the taffeta creature. Severed the cross-sectioned abyss into wafer thin slices of biological, logical tissue and…

Sometimes I hate myself.

Sometimes I hate myself too…

12

He Dives Too Deep

Philip Hoare

On 7 June 1935, eighteen-year-old Denton Welch, a slight, bespectacled, curly-haired young man who was studying art at the Goldsmith School of Art in New Cross, decided to cycle from his lodgings at 34 Croom's Hill, a neat Georgian house in Greenwich, to spend the weekend with his aunt and uncle in Leigh, Surrey.

Setting off on his trip that bright Sunday morning, Welch packed his bag. Like everything else in his life, it was assembled with a certain precision, if not fussiness. 'I took very little with me, only pyjamas, tooth-brush, shaving things, and the creamy-white ivory comb which I had bought with my grandfather's present to me. I was very fond of this comb, so I wrapped it carefully in the pyjamas and stowed it with the other things in the shiny black bag that was fastened on the back of the seat'.

He pushed his bike up the hill, on the western side of the park, a street he knew well, with its houses shouldered together as if to stop themselves from tumbling into the nearby river. He looked over the park and its Spanish chestnuts to Greenwich's grand naval buildings, the winding Thames and the Isle of Dogs. Then, having reached the top of the hill at Blackheath, where the land levelled out into a scrubby common, he got back on his bike and rode down through south London.

He enjoyed the sense of escape from the city, with the prospect of the open country ahead. He cycled on towards Bromley and Coulsdon, where suburbia seeped into commuter belt and where the city's psychic casualties were housed in sprawling water-tower asylums. As the cars and lorries sped past, he remembered how his father used to call him 'Safety First', because he was so wary about crossing the road.

Moments later, his world was overturned. A motorist ran into him from behind, throwing him off his bike and into the verge. As he lay there in the grass, he heard 'a voice through a great cloud of agony and sickness'. It was a policeman, asking over and again, 'What is your name? Where do you live? Where were you going?' 'I could hear the fright in his voice'.

He was in a new, transformed world of pain. 'Rich clouds of what seemed to be a combination of ink and velvet soot kept belching over me, soaking into me, then melting away. Bright little points of light glittered all down the front of the liquid man kneeling beside me… the earth swung, hovered, leaving my feet in the air and my head far below. I was overcome and drowned in waves of sickness and blackness…'

What follows is a series of dream-like episodes in which he is sucked into the medical system of the nineteen-thirties, a tyrannical regime. He is helpless, supine, submissive — a patient because that is what he must be, the price he must pay for his care. In turn, he is subject to the whims of nurses too bound up in their routines to consider the subject of their work. 'I was caught and could never escape the terrible natural law'. In this new world, he even has to learn to speak again. 'The words came out of my mouth. Some of them were slightly incorrect, others a little fantastic.'

His body is invaded, uninvited. A catheter is fitted; he is fed from a pap bowl, bathed, or sedated, or stripped of his dressings; this is how it will be from now on. 'It seemed to me that something had happened which I had expected all my life… that I ought to accept the horror as something quite ordinary'. The art student is surrounded, not by beautiful, self-selected things, but by instruments of penetration and excision and absorption: gauze and forceps and boiled linen and kidney dishes, which I always believed where shaped to receive human organs.

The pain is so great he feels his skin will burst with it, as if he were a chrysalis in the process of metamorphosis. Only when a pair of student friends come to visit does he see what he has become. Taking a make-up mirror from one of the women, he sees his new face for the first time. His eyes are reduced to slits, an Ahabian forked cut 'like red lightning' from his forehead to his nose, his hair cut away in parts, or standing up in 'isolated curls and jagged tufts. The parts of my face that were not purple or red were dyed brilliant sulphur-yellow… I felt made up for some stage performance'. But it is a performance for which the only audience is himself.

✵

WHEN IT FIRST HAPPENED, time stopped still. Or perhaps it went into reverse, spooling back to excise the moment of impact from my memory. My life stopped, and restarted, dissolved in adrenaline. Spaces fell out of my brain. I was in a foreign place, I didn't know where. I knew I had a good friend in the same city, but I couldn't remember her name or even her face. But just as I had no memory, neither did I feel any pain. I stood there, over a dark pool of blood in the gutter, asking for water. When it came, I used it to try and wash the stains out of my favourite shirt. I worried that I'd missed my last train home. Most of all, I worried about my bike, lying abandoned on the kerb where it had skewed beneath me. Someone promised to take care of it.

The darkness of the summer night seemed to swallow up the scene. I don't know how I got to the hospital, although I do remember someone called Adam, a security guard, being at my side, and wanting to be hugged by him, as if to arrest the momentum of the crash still reverberating through my body. As I waited on a bed to be seen, the geriatric woman opposite me had taken off her blouse — it was one of the hottest nights of the year — and had exposed her yellowy breasts. She cried, 'Why won't someone come and help me?', like a line from a war poem whose author I couldn't recall. I thought of my own mother in intensive care, wired up in a darkened ward, instruments beeping out the sonic fathoms of her descent like a submarine.

✲

BEFORE HIS ACCIDENT, he was a young man, capable of anything. Now his life was mapped out in a dwindling inevitability, driven by illness into extreme self-analysis. He delights in his selfish, unworthy thoughts, as though shocking his more proper, prim, whole self.

From his London hospital, which can do nothing more for him, Welch is sent to the desultory resort of Broadstairs, at southern England's easternmost edge. His bed is pulled up to the window; he feels surrounded by sea and sky. He now weighs less than five stones; barely a bag of cobbles from the beach. The expanse of sea becomes an extension of his terror and loneliness, its emptiness 'the negation of everything living. The suck and mumble of the waves on the beach, licking and slithering and eating, filled me with a wry, fearful pleasure'. He sings to himself, not so much in consolation as in despair.

Later in the morning, his nurse will take him up to the roof where, propped up on a deckchair with a windbreak tied behind it to protect him and covered with an eiderdown, the February sun becomes warm enough for him to cast off his covers and even his pyjamas, exposing his pale flesh, acquiring a superficially healthy glow. At night he listens to the 'washing and whining' waves which have become an extension of his own body, 'the wonderful, booming, wriggling skin of the sea'. The quiet suburban houses sit back from the cliffs. This is a place where people are sent to recuperate or die. Once, a whale was washed up on this same beach, groaning and writhing as its great body lay hoicked out of the water. Someone walked into its mouth.

✵

'THERE'S NOT MUCH OF YOU', Sue the nurse says in her Bristolian accent, altogether too breezy for three o'clock in the morning, She talks and laughs out loud with no concession to the hour or a ward full of sleeping patients. Lying prone and in pain, I do not hold it against her. Still less so when, once the lights come up — in the same way as they do towards the end of a long overnight flight — she brings two rounds of toast, marmalade no butter, my reward for having survived the night. My arm is still connected to a drip, my body sustained by saline pumped into it, filling me with the sea inside. We lie in our beds, the bycatch of the life going on outside. Ours is a temporary surrogate society to which anyone might belong in their degrees of misfortune. Everything strives to appear normal. Everyone is pretending.

I'm wheeled into the darkened x-ray room to be spread out on a table, unetherised, examined for whatever might have happened within the sack of my skin. In a matter-of-fact, sympathetic voice, the radiographer tells me my left hand, with which I write, is fractured, and will require a cast. Later, illicitly open the envelope containing the disk on which they are preserved, I will look at the images, as if I were spying on my own inner self. Sliding it into my machine, I see the shadowy me, ribs and phalanges in the mist, clouds and bones flickering and floating in the depths like the luminous skeleton of a whale threaded and fissured with skeins of ghostly coral.

PRONOUNCED FIT TO LIVE UNSUPPORTED, albeit in a state of semi-invalidity, Welch moves into a kind of rural suburbia in the Home Counties. He is well enough to get back on his bike, although the reality is that his body will never recover. Riding around the Kentish countryside one afternoon, he sees some teenage boys by the river, diving from the locks and lounging in the sun. He observes their dark wet hair and the V-shaped tans on their chests. They seem to perform for him, these boys.

> 'Quick, Ginger', his friend yelled unnecessarily to him, 'get your clothes off and come and dive off the high platform'.
>
> Ginger disappeared into the long grass by a mound, and I caught glimpses of clothes being pulled into the air, and the sudden dead whiteness of his shoulders. He rushed out of the grass, dead pearly white except for his freckled face, with little, lumpy, rather over-developed stomach and pectoral muscles. A rather broken up, not pretty, surface fussiness. Different from his friend's smooth lazy-looking body.
>
> Pulling his mouth back and showing his teeth in a wild, mad, excited gesture, he rushed at the water and dived, going so deep and straight down that his legs almost turned a somersault.
>
> 'He dives too deep,' I said to the friend.

Afterwards the boys lie on the grass beside him.

> The first boy lay flat on his back and half shut his eyes. He looked charmingly coarse and young-animalish now, with thick brown neck, smooth arms and hairs round each brown-red nipple. Ginger turned his extremely white and knobbly back to me and almost bent over his friend, talking to him about his work, and how he had been late because he had been staying at home, pressing his trousers for the dance that night.

✵

I FOUND WELCH'S BOOK, *A Voice Through a Cloud,* at a jumble sale in a suburban church hall when I was a teenager in the nineteen-seventies. I'd never heard of him, but his writing spoke to me, out of a place in which beauty might be preserved, and yet slowly decay, wasted and lonely, where what one used to be and what one might become were one and the same thing.

Welch invents himself out of that world. In his private theatre of elegant, confined interiors, embellished with crystal lustres and carved angels, he dresses in a cassock, his thin limbs poking out of its cuffs and hem. He paints and draws entwined shells and wide-eyed cats, mermaid-like sea creatures impaled on thorns and disembodied hands holding vases, all floating in an amniotic world of their own.

Faces sprout from cone-like shapes or stare as blind-eyed as statuary; landscapes become dreamy, disturbing stage sets of follies decorated with emblematic, anthropomorphic trees. These fantastical images were an alternative to the apocalyptic war going on over his head, the clouds dealing death, indiscriminately, from above. They feed into his writing like his dreams. The right people read his work. He is published, and, for a few short years in the nineteen-forties, achieves a certain sort of subtle fame.

Wreathed in the glamour of illness in a neo-romantic manner, he is photographed lying on a fur rug, surrounded by shells, looking languidly, half dead, back at the camera, seeing saw himself as if in an out-of-body experience, as if he were back on the road, back broken, or in his hospital bed, 'two eyes looking down on my empty room, on my silent velvet bed, on all my pretty things, and knowing that I shall never use them again. I think of them floating into other people's homes and being used for a hundred years from hence. I think of wars and torture and the blackest sins of power. I think of babies and all the screaming life of eternity. This is the horrible, beautiful immortality that we've been looking for. The never-ending of our race on earth.'

✡

I WALK DOWN TO THE SEA WALL and defying advice, climb over, pull off my clothes, and wade into the sea up to my waist. The water is warm, surging around my body. It wants to bear me up and away. Enticed, I attempt to immerse myself more, then realise my folly. My cast would quickly become a soggy mass; I imagine my broken bones flopping out of it, flapping uselessly like an unhomed hermit crab. Maybe I'll be like this forever. What if someone removed my skeleton entirely, or replaced it with that of a dog, or of a dolphin? Perhaps this just another transformation.

Back at home, I photograph myself in the mirror, through the mirror, cropping the image of my cracked face to my right forehead, temple and eye. My pale eye looks out through the lurid bruises as they ripen and blush the way a piece of fruit decays. Stitched in electric blue, my face changes over these days, in a filmic sequence, from bright red to magenta and green, developing as it seeks to repair, to return me to me. I think I look like Aladdin Sane. I see my skin blush unnaturally pink, methylated purple and iodine yellow, an exquisite decadent flower, blooming beneath my skin. I ache with sympathy for my teenage self. It is the last time I looked beautiful.

'I WAS HARD AND BRIGHT AND UNCONTAMINATED'. At night he hears dogs barking and birds singing like 'sad future souls'. When he looks at what he has written, 'something was wrong with it. There is always something wrong with writing'. Like his body.

Semi-paraplegic, impotent, and in constant pain, Denton Welch died on 30 December, 1948. The last photograph shows him wearing a tweed suit and polo-neck jumper, his cherubic face now preternaturally lined, a chronic frown on his choirboy brow. He is sitting outside, his arm around one of his baroque wooden angels which he is cleaning. It is almost as big as he is.

Its wings arch around him, as if it were his own gravestone. It is the last time he looked beautiful.

13

more flinching

Heather Phillipson

it came

because I came
through stacks of airport
terminals railway arches security
checkpoints tunnels a revolving door
into the hotel lobby's free wifi HOTSPOT
with Chopin in the backcloth making everything personal
on tickertape & CNN's mouths
permanently overhead leeching terror
into the common cerebrum where chips
get lodged and served with a side
of forcible emotion because
I already came from interspaced days
and nights of recurring feelings
of my dead dog and grandmother
spreading into all stories in newspapers
of exploding torsos exploding dogs
replacement dogs women griefs
close-up eye-witnesses and already
in my body getting bigger and taking over
until passivity was an absurdity
and wasn't it always and will be

I
came
close to his
WET dog's eye
& a FAT tear shared
animal PAIN sloshed &
seeped in between us—
"darling I'm sorry you
were born a dog &
people notice it"

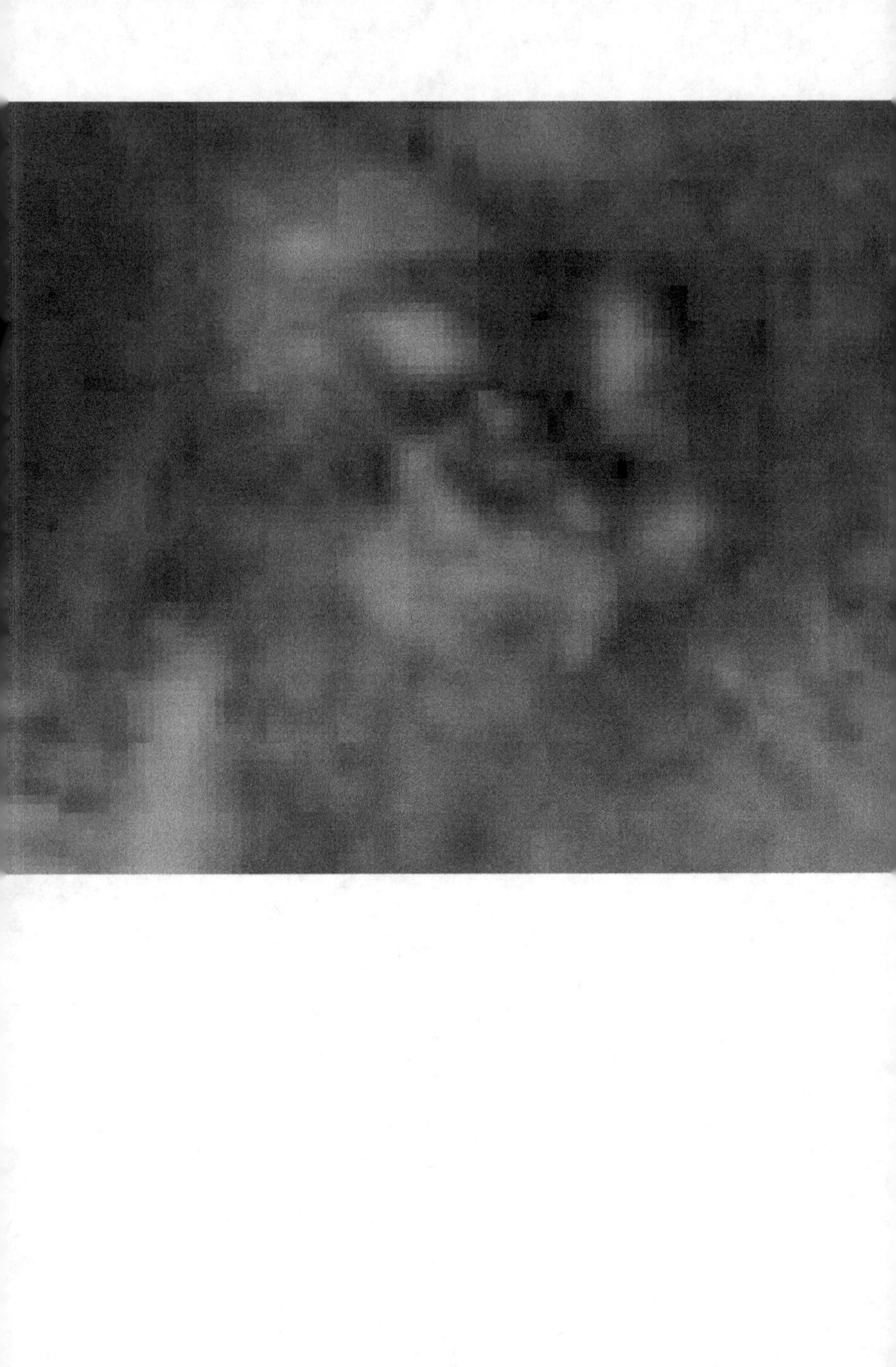

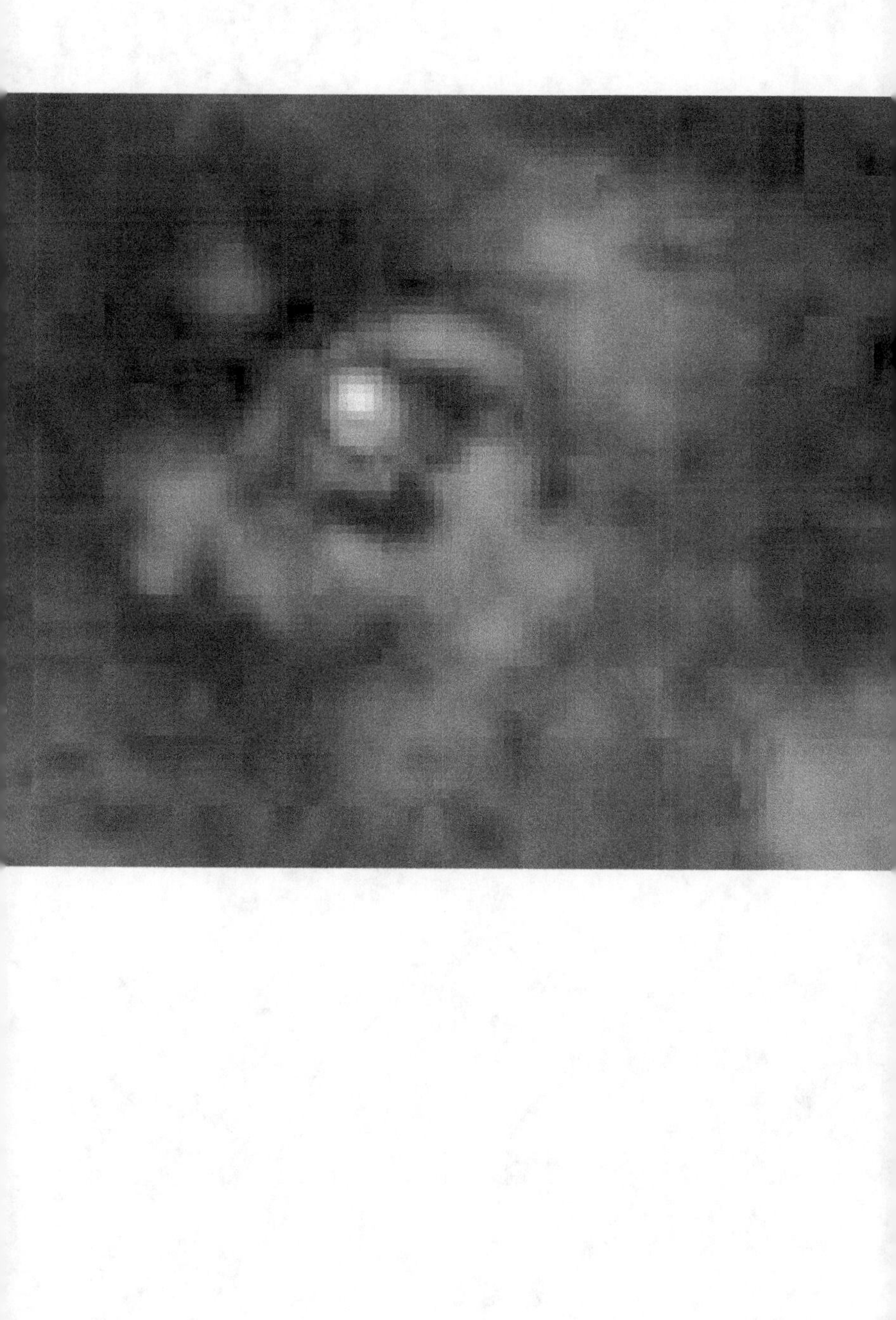

LISTEN

1

oh
that
that's just the snivel of an average day
in which every neutron feels charged with significance
awaiting a kind of atomic birthing
like a caesarian watermelon

ready

to begin at the beginning or
for instance
'universal time'
is running
(or I am)
already
6 seconds behind schedule

or just

outside Paris
the kilogram is
losing weight
at a rate of multi-nanograms
from the paranoid sweating

or is it

the sky flopping straight down
into our sewer system?

let's not

worry identity
between the basic elements
we wouldn't want to

wear them
out or
for instance

THE FIRST RUDE BOMBING
HAS STARTED

with naming
which sets off a disconcertingly translatable
international standard

based on promotional identication
in other words
the selves I inhabit

meaning

(imagine calling the self
for the first time

imagine its first 'bikini wax'
imagine circulating the self's 'clitoris'
(which, the self senses, barely
scratches the self's 'surface')
imagine the self's 'ball-sacks'
having their first self-message against its first Lycra®
imagine the self's first 'day'
at the disappointing 'multiplex'
its 'aeroplane'/'food' premiere
imagine slamming the self
into the 'Atlantic' from 30,000 'metres'
its 'organs' hacked by 'ice-water'
getting 'carried away' or just 'drowned' in 'self-pity'
imagine the self shot thru with 'narcotics'
its 'veins' blackening while,
on YouTube, a 'man' is decapitated
while the self imagines itself as another 'self'
or 'thousands' of them
self-sealed in a 'hell' of self-making
why not imagine
the 'day' creeping down
the self's 'complexion'
the 'moon' creeping up on it
            "ho-ho!"
the 'tricks' the self plays on the self
so it doesn't have to imagine
dumping the 'self' on the 'dump'
watching its selves self-seeding
            astride 'rotting haddocks')

erotic haddocks

2 COME ON IN, WE'VE BEEN EXPECTING YOU

like a clue
we found PEOPLE
in the KITCHEN
in the SUICIDE VEST
with the KALASHNIKOV

such beautiful, desperate weapons
their faces

had to be covered
so we didn't fall in love
piteously
with the self-same wretchedness
we see in mirrors

a worryingly familiar scene
we've lived in will live in
the carnage
going on
behind closed doors

being told, regurgitatingly, 'you only get one shot!'

but is it true
you only get one shot
when you get a loaded magazine
& plenty more
where that came from
in the MUNITIONS DEPOT
which I picture in Arizona,
right beside a render farm
and to the left
THE CLOUD
that backs up
and up and up
up
to where
are there edges, Bobby?

INTELLIGENCE tells us
to test the power of names
by naming things, for one thing
to name is to guarantee the end
like a starting pistol
BANG

you name
it it's
smithereens

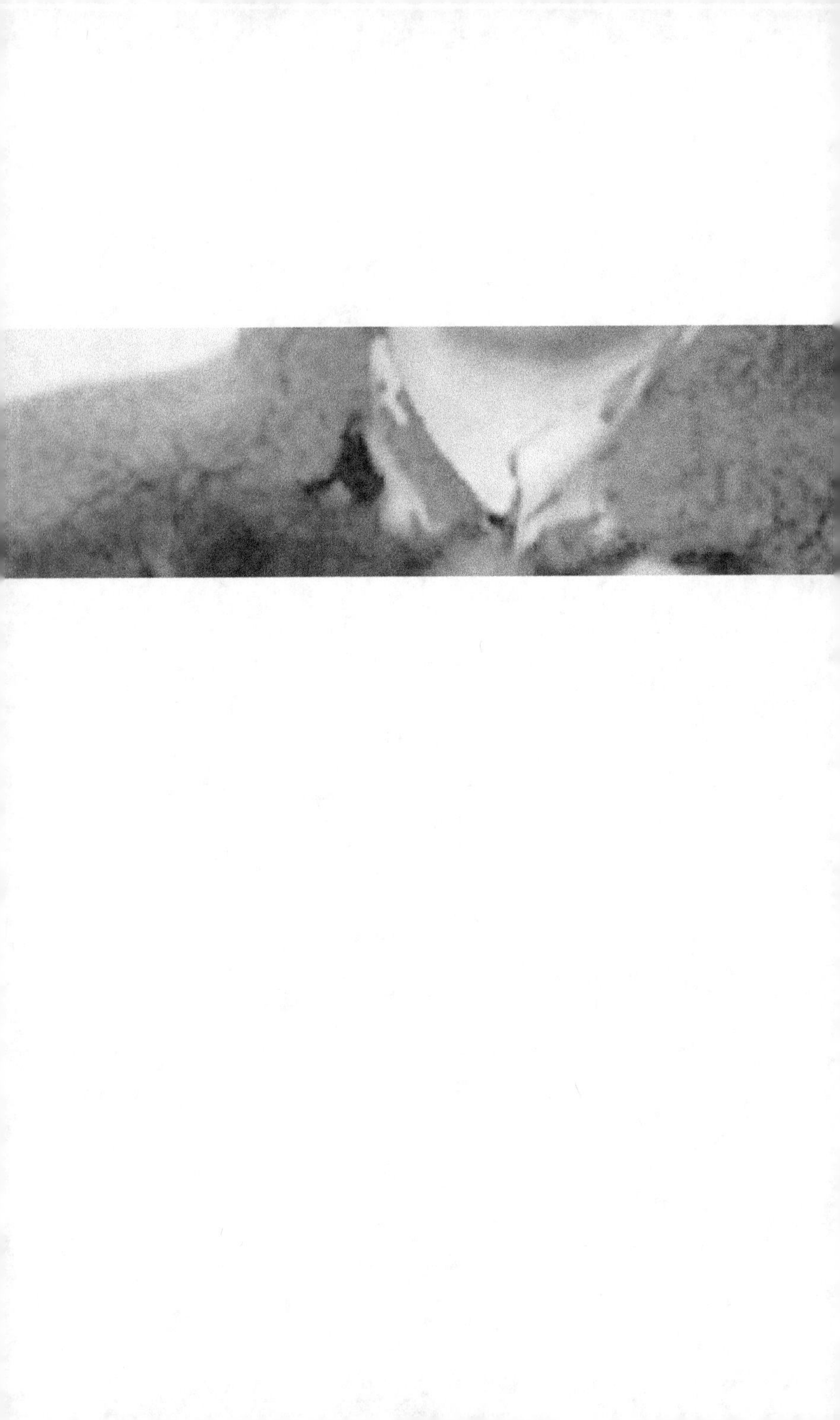

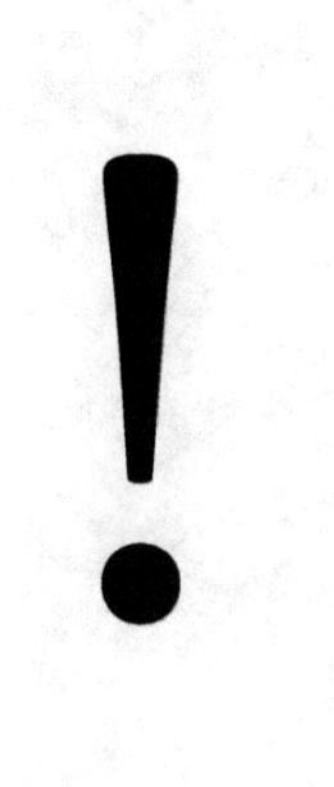

3

do you smell
the hints

1 HEAD
1 SPINAL CORD
1 GUT-FULL

your task is to
sniff them out before
they thrash
the sash window
& ricochet
off our roof rack

I'll make it up to you, darling, in dog biscuits
in the afterlife

in makeshift dark
we can burst apart
any body
& no body
stays intact for long anyway
we reasoned

'shame is inventive'
so said Nietzsche

it's the bomb that trips
the bloody brain
off

but maybe not enough
in this corner
of dawn (us)
repetitive and transparent
waiting for a bullet

•

to full-stop it

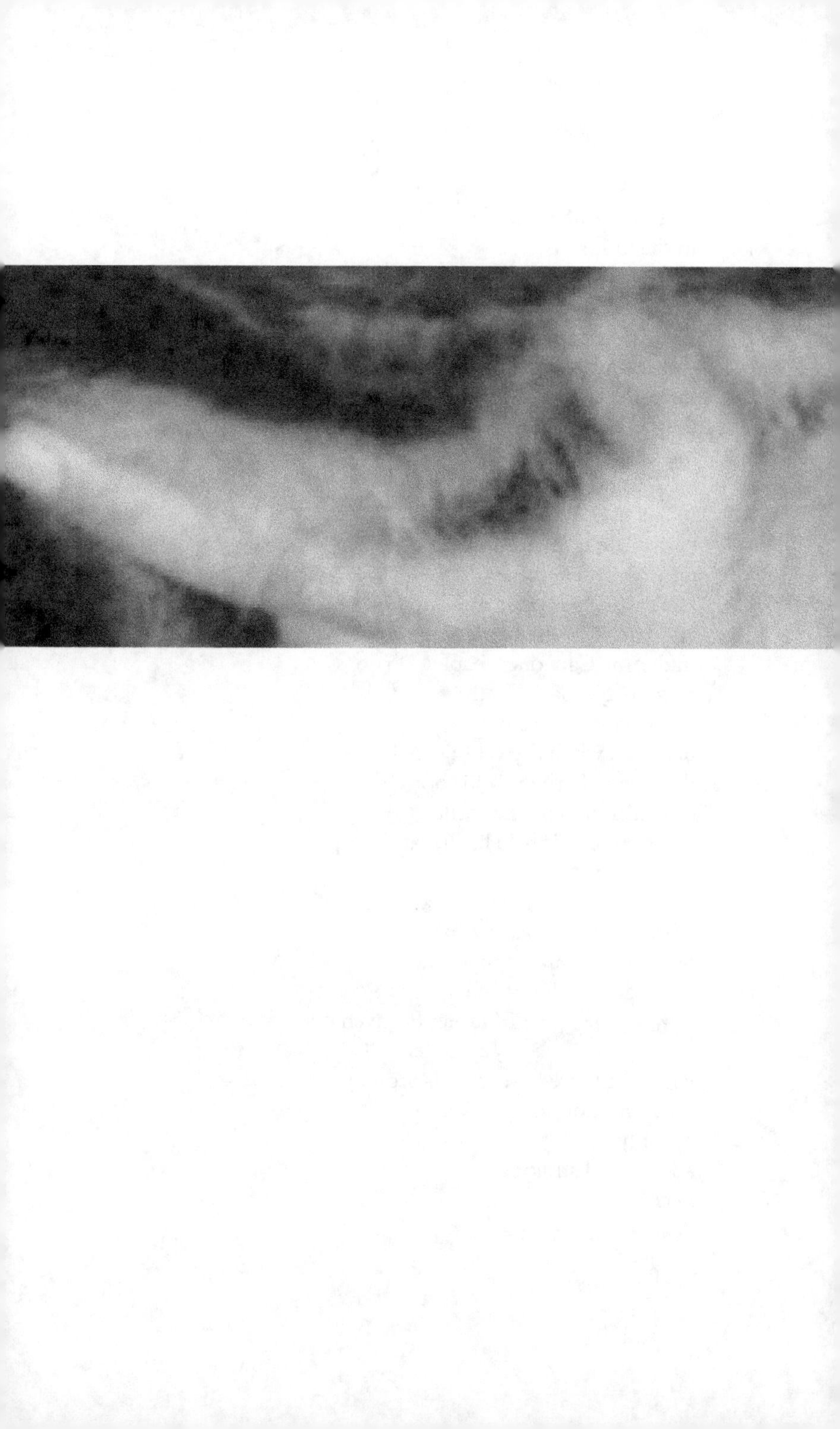

4

I am so indifferent
to the limits
of feelings
I can't tell the difference
every time someone lifts my flap
the unwashed salad
the unheated leftovers
the sanitary products are standard
but bear no relation
to what I expected
to feel overlaid
with various forms of filth
don't you sometimes feel
like getting wrapped in a dog towel
and buried in the hardening ground
under the Canadian maple? Do dogs
need to approach death
and back away from it
like I did when the vet injected
deep pentobarbital & his bowels
ejected across the floor tiles
I was there to inhale his fur and weep
for my benefit
I am not independent
of my feelings this way
of talking about feelings
has fooled each one of us
                                        I'd rather be given CBT
                                        by a border collie
when there are fewer words around
my arms around
his only
adored and stinking
neck
dead

up my nostrils

throw me in there with him everything is
in the cold
awful and I'm not OK
and without good reason
still here and

feelings

received:

DOG CRATE

thanks to Russia

5

This scene takes place in a moving casket.
Moving scenes take place in locked rooms, in claustrophobic cartons. They say that when you take a puppy home you should put it in a box just big enough for it.
Dripping with as much atmosphere as it does frantic panting.
Or maybe I'm reading too much into it.
Until you open the lid, the puppy is also not-dead.
Hear that?
Context is everything or nothing when it comes to breathing.

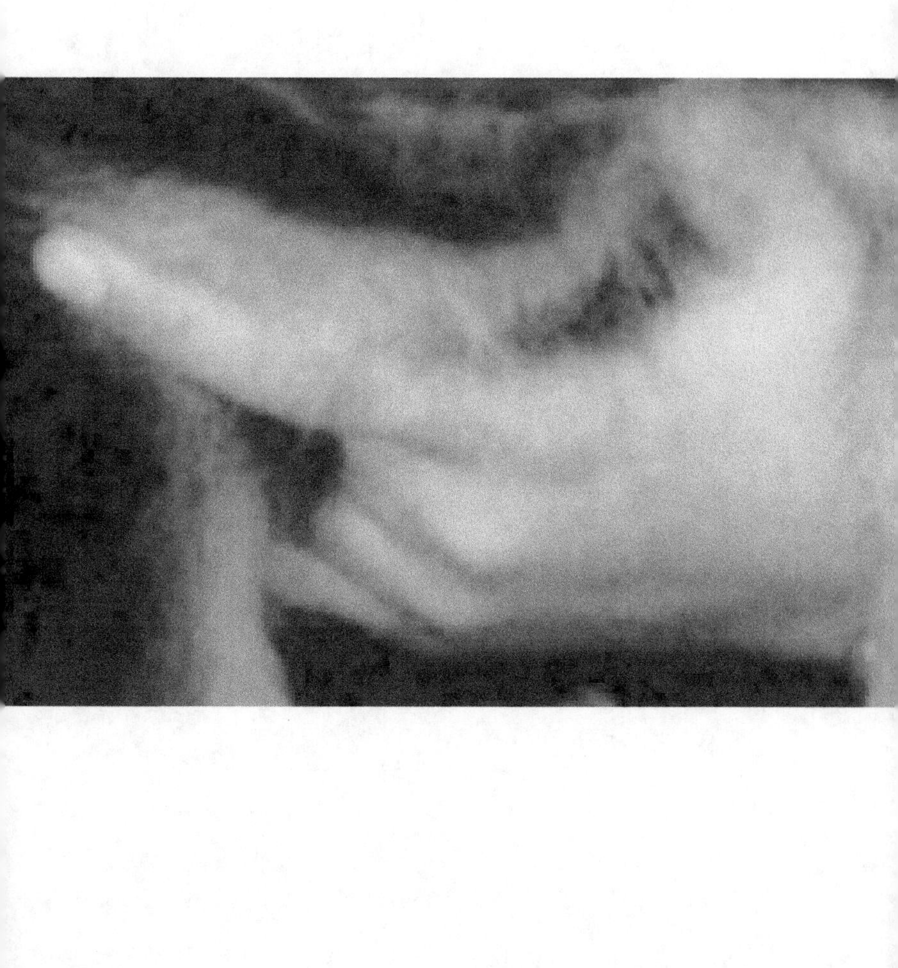

6

JUST A GENTLE REMINDER

A LOT OF WORK
goes into making sex alluring sex
is just this and that
but it seemed, for a moment, that a new
climax had been won when

even the sky fingered me
with a slobbery insistence when
we were retching with so much desire
we created a whole new atmosphere
grabbing at sex things /
using the sick bag to be actually sick in
now the shower curtain is transparent
it's a way of saying, "I want you too
to have this experience
so that we are more alike
like a sign that life struck once
in a slippy-bits marathon
that began when our eyes were magnets
yanked to each other's fully charged
crotches at a picnic
when it was essential
to make every enhancement
to our 'connection' by getting seriously indecent
beside the bluetooth wireless speaker system
until even the trees had to dash inside
to pour ice in their underpants"
while I choked up playing the scene, as we lived it,
united by our pursuit of arrhythmia or
satisfying itches to that
catchy bridge section in Chopin
(I couldn't wait to come with Chopin through his melancholic
meadow (not that I approve of background music
(I prefer to foreground the piano by massaging it loud
and all over until the top layer comes off in my hand
and the pedal squeaks for humanity
(I like to FEEL a piano as an instrument
of interruption and consciousness
(though I also like to take light swims, to get away from what I
FEEL (today I felt jellybeans
resemble kidneys))))))
which throbs like everyone grieving

7 HERE, HAVE A NEW PUPPY

said the Russians to the French
to soften the dog-loss
but mostly the dog's image the image
is the greater likeness
except we never seem to run out of images
sometimes something in an image
runs through me and that is very common
as is reading about something
that's happening to someone outside of me
until I know someone outside of me
without any knowledge
it is a test for my knowledge
to hang around until morning
practically all mornings are news to me
practically all knowledge is news to me
practically all news is images
going very fast around the world
so we have to them guzzle them
like wrapped food
— hot and on the run —
in one end and squitted out the other
[*pics or it didn't happen*]
until I'm fat with implications
and containing not a sausage

8 EAT SHIT LOVE

EAT, SHIT, LOVE

EAT SHIT, LOVE

EAT, SHIT LOVE

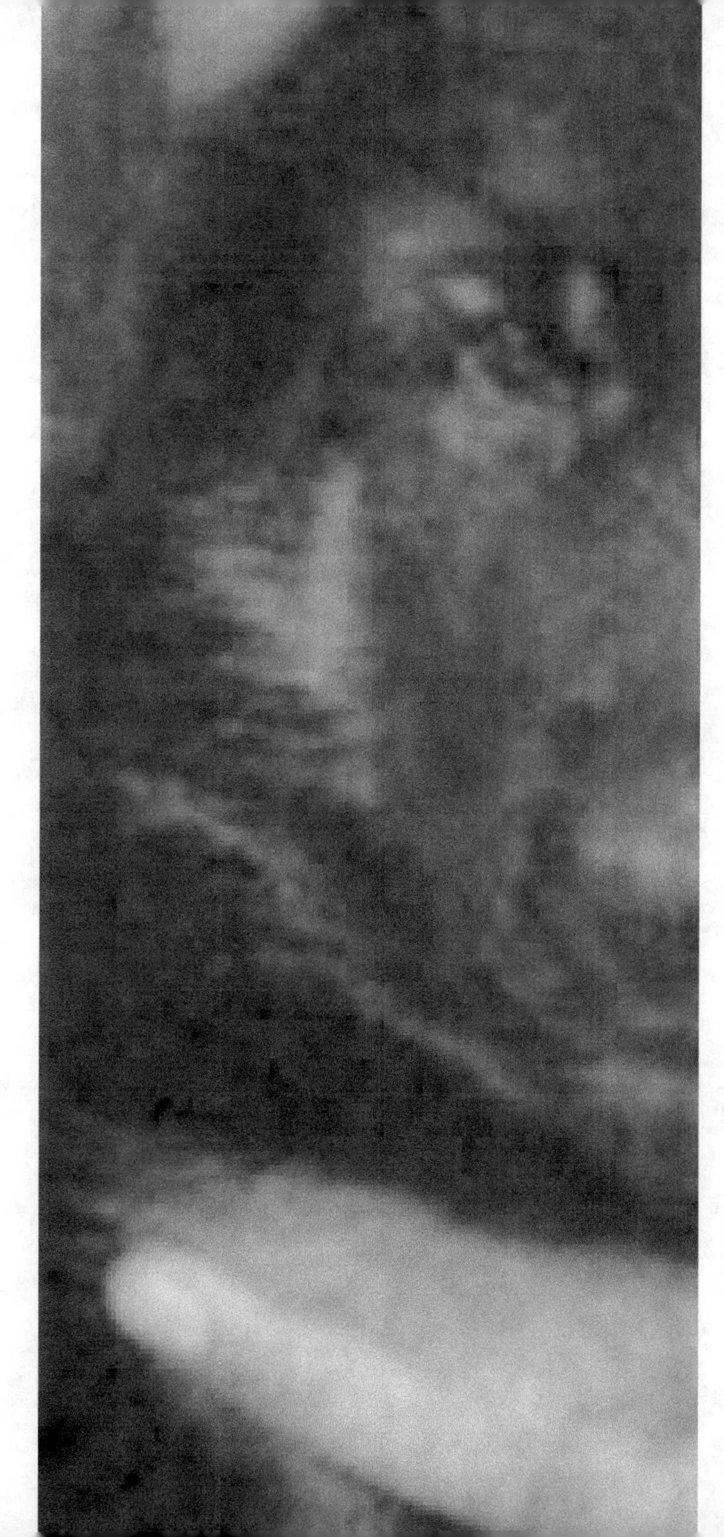

9

I love a good weepie
dog-meme as much as the next crybaby
and nauseate irregularly
when the gifs load automatically
his hairy body
into my hairy body

unfairly the dog
becomes the shape of 2.13pm
in me on a Tuesday

if we accept the world as totally fucked
there's a lot worse coming
than dog hairs in macaroni cheese dog hairs on pillows dog hairs in rented flats in bathtubs in my hair in my dog's hair in your short & curlies between my teeth in coagulant soap bars

some people are revolted
by dogs and dogs
are not up for revolting
myself, I am revolted
when dogs are lacking

what if he did lick my cheeks
by which I mean 'buttocks'
which were coated in whipped shea butter and
heavily comestible

it's obvious he's related to a father
he never knew
because we found all his needs
and perverted them
into a kind of inter-species loyalty
or the usual master-slave hierarchy

before laying down the crisp breakfast bowl
of the rest of his days
which gave us carte blanche to rush in anytime
and smother him with kisses
without getting socked in the eye
(unlike when I tried the same on Johnny (who spat my tongue
out (& no-one blamed him)))
when maybe all he wants is
just to go on
being less and less
subtle and alive
the way life becomes
very well known after its termination

10 [BCU kitchen floor, dog's body (dead), piss]

11

there are things going on
that can't be seen
in the dark
I've been told my skin
looks like an astronomical
surface stretching
from here to eternity
but how
do you see eternity
when our faces
are so close
we can't see
each other's faces
is eternity
in spitting distance
like my lower lip
you're chewing
on a park bench
like a dog grinning (do dogs grin? what
is there to grin about?)
like my eyes spit

overhearing Chopin's
Fantasie Impromptu Opus 66
the notes appear
as a real thing
outside of me
and inside of me
stopgap
maternal redemption
on that occasion
was I aroused
or sleepy or sad
or too tender
from too much missing
my grandma
in close-up
in the dark
we go too close
to the feeling
parts are
not detachable

12

If rigor mortis sets in
it means there's somebody who needs it.
It means that somebody
is drained and not awake
and deems any speckles of life unusable
and he is dead and dead
all dead in the humus
of trashed bodies shoved down there
dressed in made-up relationships.

What's your favourite part?
Mine's every part
with a maggot in it. Maggots
mean that life's still leaking.

It's like magic
when his dead voice
is nauseating
and I can't see him
so he might as well be invisible.
It's like magic when he isn't
and doesn't have anything to say
and I can't bear to listen anyway
so I just recognize my fingers / all
the injuries they've inflicted
while my skin drops off.

What's worse than a maggot
in the EAT ME
GLOVE-BOX DATES?
Does the 5-second rule apply
to something that drops dead?
Is it true he might come back
and crack open a piñata
blue alcopops, bombay mix, karaoke and a pint of nostalgia

which is like thinking in another language,
I mean, how it feels, not what it means.

Half a maggot, the memory of
mange marching across his fur
describes a lot of other feelings
the feeling that someone else is taking up the whole room
the feeling that no one could help me now
or ever whether I was on several edges
my hot core and noggin facing this hammering world
of brainlessness and sweetbreads
was always a favourite word.
I don't know what it tastes like but I know it's terrible.

a:ldskjfa:lkdgjsa
meaning
I'm so overcharged
that all I can do is literally slam
my hands/head/breasts against the keyboard.

Wherever there are
corpses there are maggots.
If we dig him up will he be wearing a jacket?
LOOK OUT
for the milkier, gentler solaces
which for all we know   for all we know
could be the wind or Chopin's noise (still hammering
the background) — who's seen it? Only its aftermath
is visible what's not visible
is the aftermath of my screaming

13 btw

each second we should shrink
romance by remaking
the thematic connection
between the people we are and
the sucking appetites we become
when we don't stick
with ourselves
we get the drift
we are also dogs
leashed to any body
that fetches & fucks us
with the same quizzical look
verging on so much need
it makes us RESTLESS
to feel better than feeling
LIFELESS

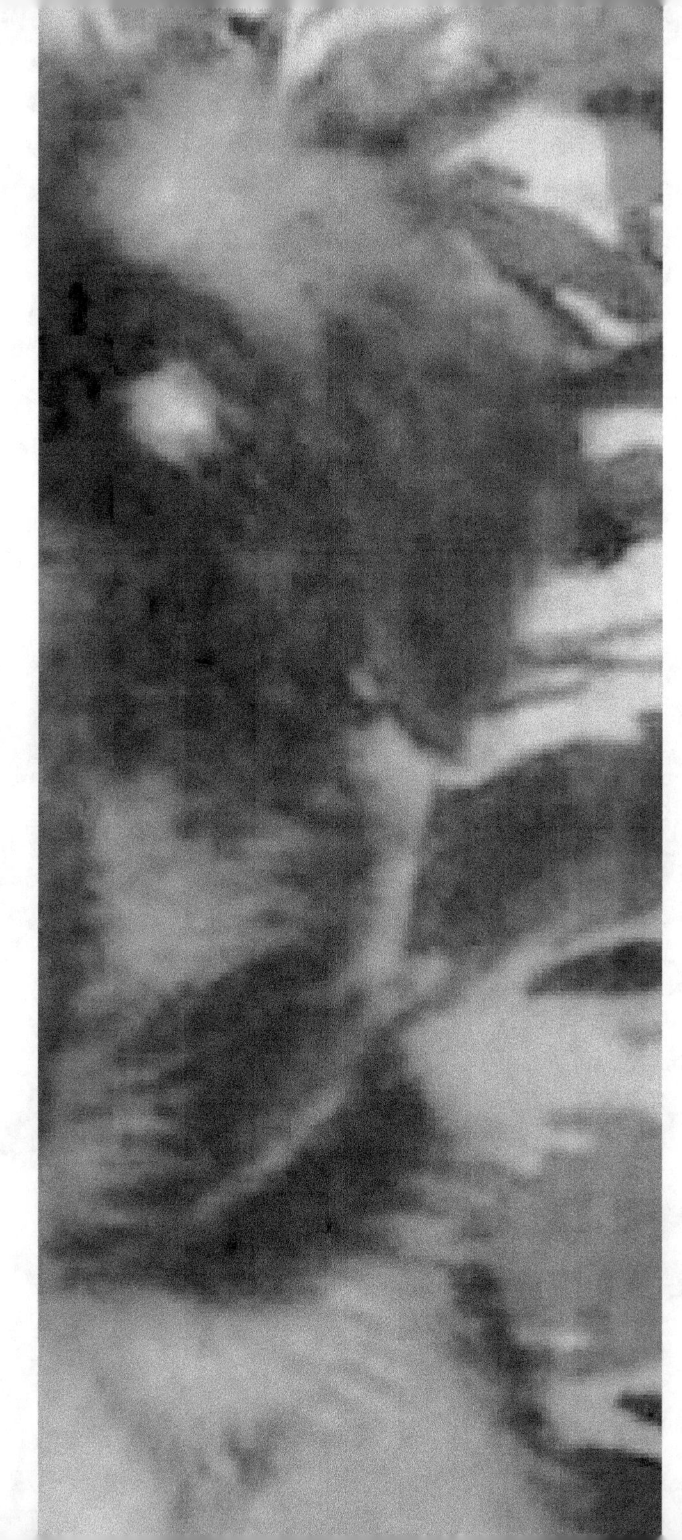

14

HEROISM

looks acceptable 'on paper'
but then, so does shit.
What's turning me on
suddenly, and simply, is grasses
picked from the earth's assholes.
You didn't see that coming
did you, the assholes
just come when the worms get digging.
I'll bet there are some
nice craters in the field right now.

As it happened, I had fully intended
to go shopping for the most
expensive most wet dog food
formed of the most tender
chunks of other species
in pouches with the same freshness
and quality you'd expect
in the field but without
any shit in the hedges
and then I got overwhelmed
by an excessive natural impulse
in new easy-spray canister, a court heard.

At first, a member of management
gave me the benefit of the doubt
and assumed I was self-adjusting.
He watched the tweaks I made
to the asshole section and was happy
to see the grasses getting attention.
But after a full 112 minutes
it became full HD my spanking
visuals and hand-gestures
were urgently not-easing
until the grasses and assholes tipped
the tone past a point
he and the members
could promote to make-up-caked mortals out for Sunday strolls
in dollops of afternoon wind like an ad for new Hair Hold.
He didn't want people getting whipped up
by the natural elements and then
sexting while other people drowned.
And then I almost drowned! the fucker.
Ironies like this suit the idea that each moment makes its own
proportions.

Read more at Scene 10

Stubbed toe. Locked door. Walked dog. Poured drink. Locked dog. Walked toe. Poured door. Stubbed dog. Stubbed toe. Locked door. Walked dog. Poured drink. Locked dog. Walked toe. Poured door. Stubbed dog. Stubbed toe. Locked door. Walked dog. Poured drink. Locked dog. Walked toe. Poured door. Stubbed dog. Stubbed toe. Locked door. Walked dog. Poured drink. Locked dog. Walked toe. Poured door. Stubbed dog. Stubbed toe. Locked door. Walked dog. Poured drink. Locked dog. Walked toe. Poured door. Stubbed dog. Stubbed toe. Locked door. Walked dog. Poured drink. Locked dog. Walked toe. Poured door. Stubbed dog. Stubbed toe. Locked door. Walked dog. Poured drink. Locked dog. Walked toe. Poured door. Stubbed dog. Stubbed toe. Locked door. Walked dog. Poured drink. Locked dog. Walked toe. Poured door. Stubbed dog. Stubbed toe. Locked door. Walked dog. Poured drink. Locked dog. Walked toe. Poured door. Stubbed dog. Stubbed toe. Locked door. Walked dog. Poured drink. Locked dog. Walked toe. Poured door. Stubbed dog. Stubbed toe. Locked door. Walked dog. Poured drink. Locked dog. Walked toe. Poured door. Stubbed dog. Stubbed toe. Locked door. Walked dog. Poured drink. Locked dog. Walked toe. Poured door. Stubbed dog. Stubbed toe. Locked door. Walked dog. Poured drink. Locked dog. Walked toe. Poured door. Stubbed dog. Stubbed toe. Locked door. Walked dog. Poured drink. Locked dog. Walked toe. Poured door. Stubbed dog. Stubbed toe. Locked door. Walked dog. Poured drink. Locked dog. Walked toe. Poured door. Stubbed dog. Stubbed toe. Locked door. Walked dog. Poured drink. Locked dog. Walked toe. Poured door. Stubbed dog. Stubbed toe. Locked door. Walked dog. Poured drink. Locked dog. Walked toe. Poured door. Stubbed dog. Stubbed toe. Locked door. Walked dog. Poured drink. Locked dog. Walked toe. Poured door. Stubbed dog. Stubbed toe. Locked door. Walked dog. Poured drink. Locked dog. Walked toe. Poured door. Stubbed dog. Stubbed toe. Locked door. Walked dog. Poured drink. Locked dog. Walked toe. Poured door. Stubbed dog. Stubbed toe. Locked door. Walked dog. Poured drink. Locked dog. Walked toe. Poured door. Stubbed dog. Stubbed toe. Locked door. Walked dog. Poured drink. Locked dog. Walked toe. Poured door. Stubbed dog. Stubbed toe. Locked door. Walked dog. Poured drink. Locked dog. Walked toe. Poured door. Stubbed dog. Stubbed toe. Locked door. Walked dog. Poured drink. Locked dog. Walked toe. Poured door. Stubbed dog. Stubbed toe. Locked door. Walked dog. Poured drink. Locked dog. Walked toe. Poured door. Stubbed dog. Stubbed toe. Locked door. Walked dog. Poured drink. Locked dog. Walked toe. Poured door. Stubbed dog. Stubbed toe. Locked door. Walked dog. Poured drink. Locked dog. Walked toe. Poured door. Stubbed dog. Stubbed toe. Locked door. Walked dog. Poured drink. Locked dog. Walked toe. Poured door. Stubbed dog. Stubbed toe. Locked door. Walked dog. Poured drink. Locked dog. Walked toe. Poured door. Stubbed dog. Stubbed toe. Locked door. Walked dog. Poured drink. Locked dog. Walked toe. Poured door. Stubbed dog. Stubbed toe. Locked door. Walked dog. Poured drink. Locked dog. Walked toe. Poured door. Stubbed dog. Stubbed toe. Locked door. Walked dog. Poured drink. Locked dog. Walked toe. Poured door. Stubbed dog. Stubbed toe. Locked door. Walked dog. Poured drink. Locked dog. Walked toe. Poured door. Stubbed dog. Stubbed toe. Locked door. Walked dog. Poured drink. Locked dog. Walked toe. Poured door. Stubbed dog. Stubbed toe. Locked door. Walked dog. Poured drink. Locked dog. Walked toe. Poured door. Stubbed dog. Stubbed toe. Locked door. Walked dog. Poured drink. Locked dog. Walked toe. Poured door. Stubbed dog. Stubbed toe. Locked door. Walked dog. Poured drink. Locked dog. Walked toe. Poured door. Stubbed dog. Stubbed toe. Locked door. Walked dog. Poured drink. Locked dog. Walked toe. Poured door. Stubbed dog. Stubbed toe. Locked door. Walked dog. Poured drink. Locked dog.

16

HOPE THIS FINDS YOU

√ just getting to shops
& back
with/out panic attack

17 because

the future
sounds like bionic houseflies
murdering all competitors in a hands-free / clean-up version
and then reproducing themselves
as world leaders.
Would you rather hose down
yesterday with a stiff chemical
or suck up tomorrow
with your raw eyelashes?
What shall we do
with our ticking stash
of ambition? Blow it up
like the bloated men
who manufactured this whole scenario
in their dreams of being
less boring. Even in their sleep
they are vigorously
scouring our passages. While tomorrow
doesn't amount to much
(until lined up in cross hairs
inside a zoom lens)
our USP is we always clean tomorrow
blindfolded — then, for every hour
after dark, we add another
protective layer – by tomorrow,
we're BIG on cushioning.
ooooooooooooooooo
Sagging energy levels hit early
and later stages since
the PR around just-getting-by
is not EXCITING
but the Prime Minister
won't pass away, tragically,
the chance to apply
an exfoliating mitt
to a hi-stakes battleground
here & here

in your living room
where the winner
is the party with the greatest feel
for tragedy which makes everything go
UP
especially numbers
of voters and corpses flying machines blood pressure eyebrows high-pitch drones high-security fences drug-use incredulity pizza-sales police-presence mistrust top shelf one arm I am reaching for the Dettox

18

what's NEW

is ONE SIZE
FITS ALL dogs'
body-armour with
ballistic-/stab-resistancy
won't suit the dog
but she'll get used
to velcro flaps
feeling instagrammable
like a wrap-around layer
over the layer over
the layers she was born wearing
like a layer of wet lycra
y'know, soiled swimsuits
and then a tougher layer
that leaves her free
to shit and sniff
ammunition
NEVER MIND
a dog's head
should be free
to believe life is all meat & balls & nasal digression
PLEASE
when she bites the big one
from a shot
to the cranium
REMEMBER
you treated her like a cheap safety vest
against survival instincts

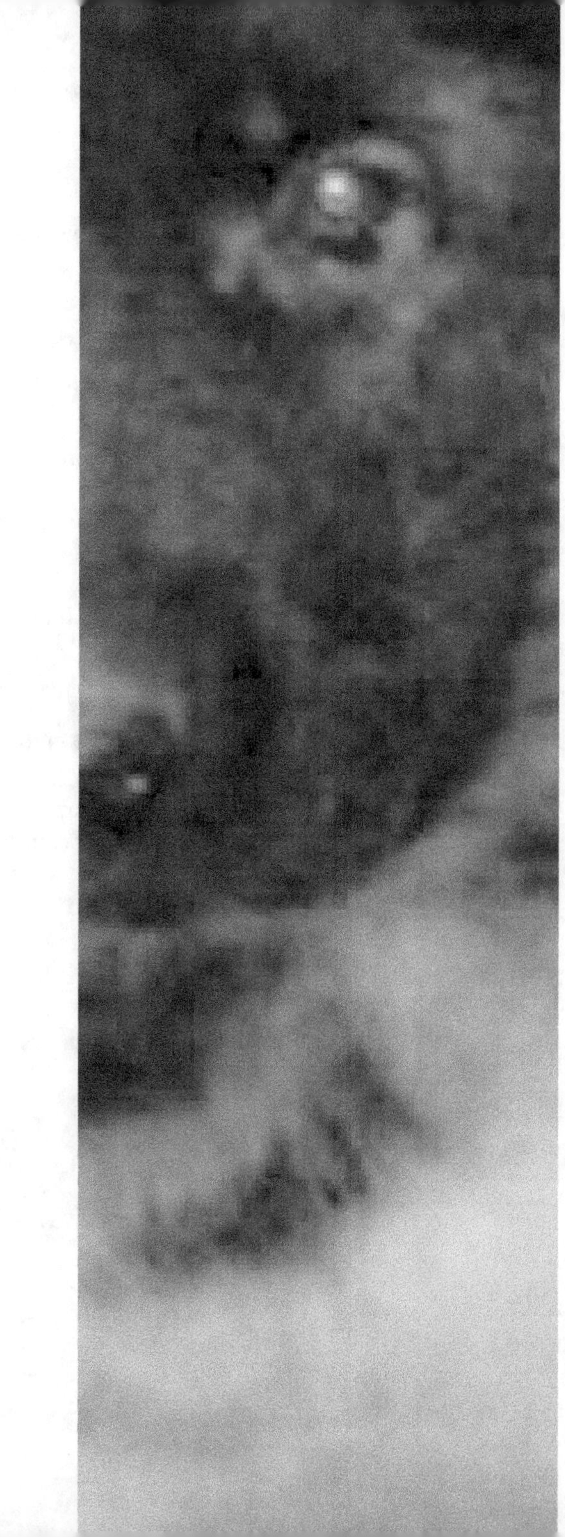

Me again. Developments.
                    The gin's gone.
                    I know an answer when I see it.
From writing emails.
                    My head hurts.
To the ghosts of dead sniffer dogs.

Have you ever seen a trembler in motion?
A trembler is a piece of jewellery.
                    The teeth ache from grinding.
Stones mounted on wires so fine they quiver.
                    Their firmness was my only
                    consolidation.
Once they're gone.
                    There's no getting them back again.

Harsh words are spoken.
       As if to a dog.
                    The dog's got hold of the wrong end
                    of the stick.
I mention my face because I am made that way.
                    Get out while you can.
This soothing friend will tame it.

Because all people are homesick.
                    This will all end badly.

Contact with actual hot & cold skin.
                                        I have the body of a wise person.
A superior achievement.
                                        Until my mouth opens.

But what if you just don't have time.
                                        For all that lying down that dogs do.
What about the 1.3 million gin and tonics.
                                        I'm not drinking to try and forget.
                                        Everything bad that's ever happened.

The lack of difference is so powerful.

At first they said.
Then they said.
                                        Don't work your glutes.
                                        You haven't worked your glutes
                                        enough.
My head hurts. Have you ever seen a trembler in motion?
Until there was so much beauty comin' out ma ass.
                                        I was literally dyyying.

There is still TIME.
                                        To come a long way from what we feel.
Start laying the groundwork.
Music is, in fact, the dog's bollocks.
                                        Crack open the hobnobs.
                                        Turn up Chopin.
                        So is the dog.
Get over it.

20

you can catch me on the

FLOOR / DOG / SYRINGE
periphery of the dying
and dead scene

FACE (FEMALE)
maybe my whole life
carting sensations to the centre
mopping shit up with towels

SKULL / COFFIN
(there are feelings for these things)
while public petting

CAR / PLANE / ROCKET
bodies leak it's no surprise
what I give away

ONE DROPLET
you can have
when the vet twirls off
to deal with some bloody business
in a kitchen

KNIFE / GUN
the hug-a-corpse scene
gets deep in the hold
of what I am

PARTY POPPER / WASTEBIN
is what I've not yet been

fyi

21

You can also use your smartphone
to select an element of the universe.
Whichever element shouts
loudest from the shelves
I can't see the ends of.
END OF
outer space! has it ever seemed more humdrum?

Yet there is something to be said
for just getting all your shopping
inside the supermarket
    when you enter
        the lights thump back causing a chain reaction
            of never-ending particles I am not in a panic
                in the supermarket modelled on the
                    glove-box format in which you can
                        manipulate bodies in a separate atmosphere
                            whacking grim jazzy monotonous and while
                                scrolling have say not only a micro-nap
                                    but also a micro-wank into this
                                        multi-use j-cloth.
                                            Huh,

parallel perks in a frigid climate.
Even if you didn't get a good feeling on Skype
there is something to be said for feelings
because there is no escaping
the chinks which keep weeping
and becoming disfigurements, I think.
I have exceeded my allowance
of first and last-minute impressions
all crafted locally and always excusing themselves under a duvet.

After he died I saw him everywhere
under a soiled towel on the kitchen lino.
And then I saw it was just the trumped-up nub
that lives inside of me
brought for slaughter.
NO to melodrama.
Though I wouldn't like to have people
actually see let alone visit my interior
nothing is isolated in me nothing is isolated in the universe
nothing does not involve me in many public acts
I don't have time for pricks in suits pointing fingers at each other.

Everything is getting later.
I could cock up the end with the beginning
until I flatline and still in some form
like plastic in the ocean which breaks down into such small segments that pieces of plastic from a one-litre plastic bottle could end up on every mile of beach across the universe
be kicking about and linked to everywhere.

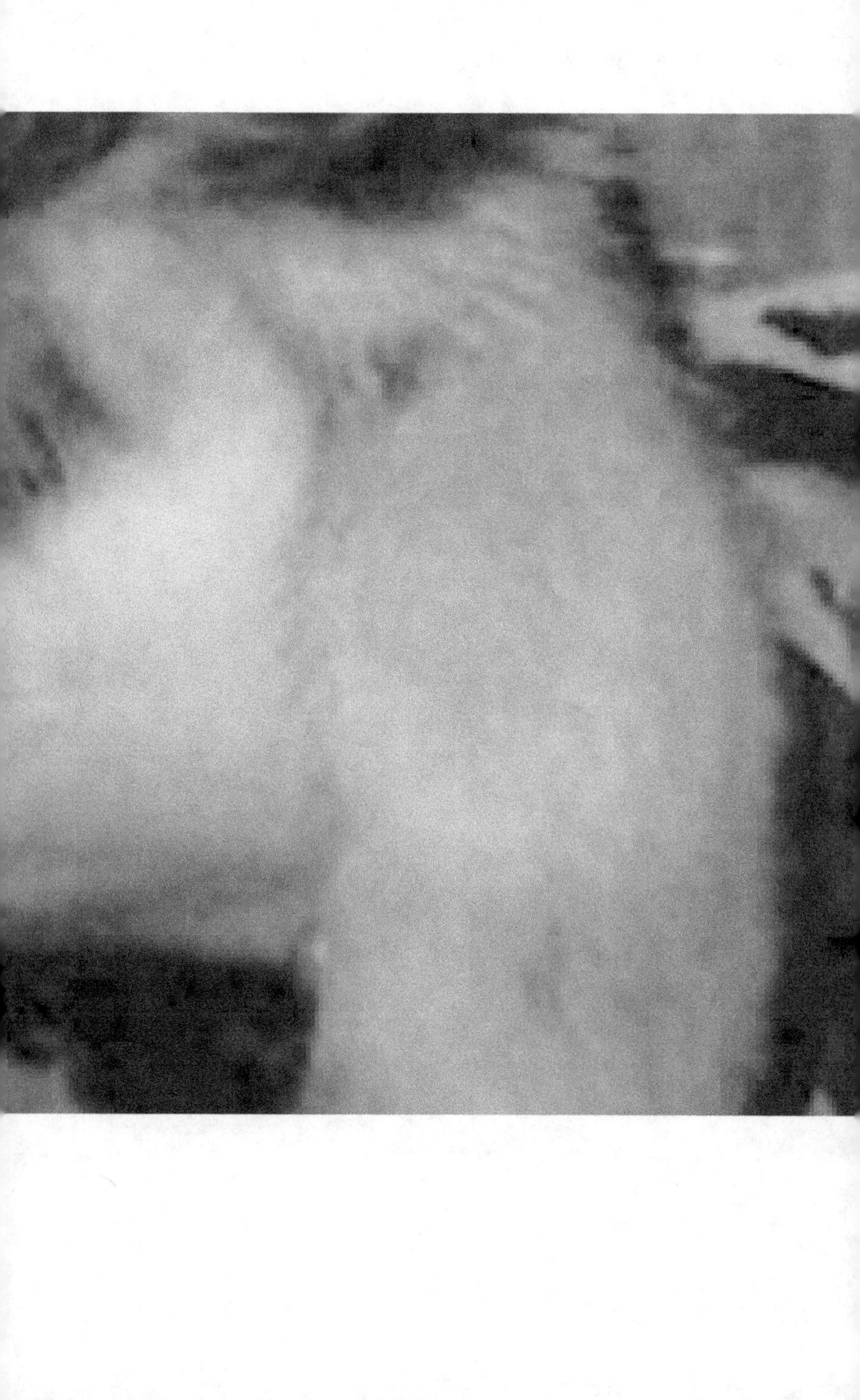

22

Actually, we live in heaven.
Eau de toilettes. Nibbles. You manhandling
the dog-food with your firmest hands on.
Aren't eyes are brilliant.
Maybe even better than the dream of grass blowing.
Ha! The sky just opened up, betraying
much more of the mystery of brainstorms.
What a triumph our human state
and by extension the world around us
is getting loved-up on the cardinal aorta.
Touch my pulse to make it official.
Probably just been to the lido, hasn't it, the compulsive splosher.
Remember eye-sex over the microwave.
Remember champagne & valium.
Let's relax a sec and recharge our selfies.
Repeated ideas massage the limbic system.
One non-lithium zeitkeeper, booted to completion.
Until, at some hour, my oomph
becomes sensuous becomes lascivious
accretions exploding the centres over
and over to the extremities. Then there's manufacturing water
from hydrogen, hyperbole
from early autumn,
the retina as a tough/ fluffy carpet,
creating an indoor potato farm
fertilised by my own excrement.
Inhale: the high street hums of fried sentiment.
Here we go! — tuning in to the sub-cellular
molecular feedback loop
of our circadian pacemakers
sounding like literally adios.

NO

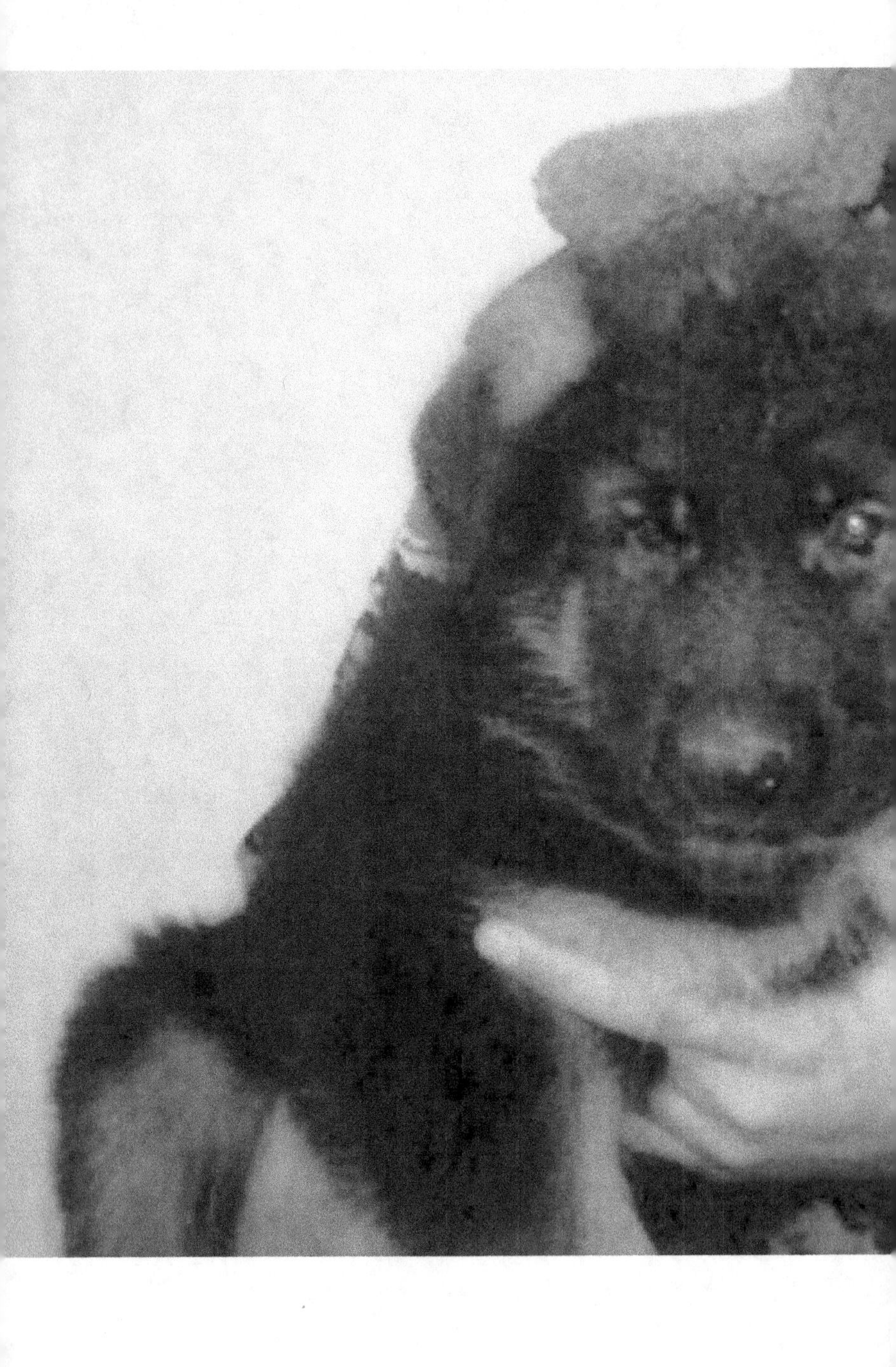

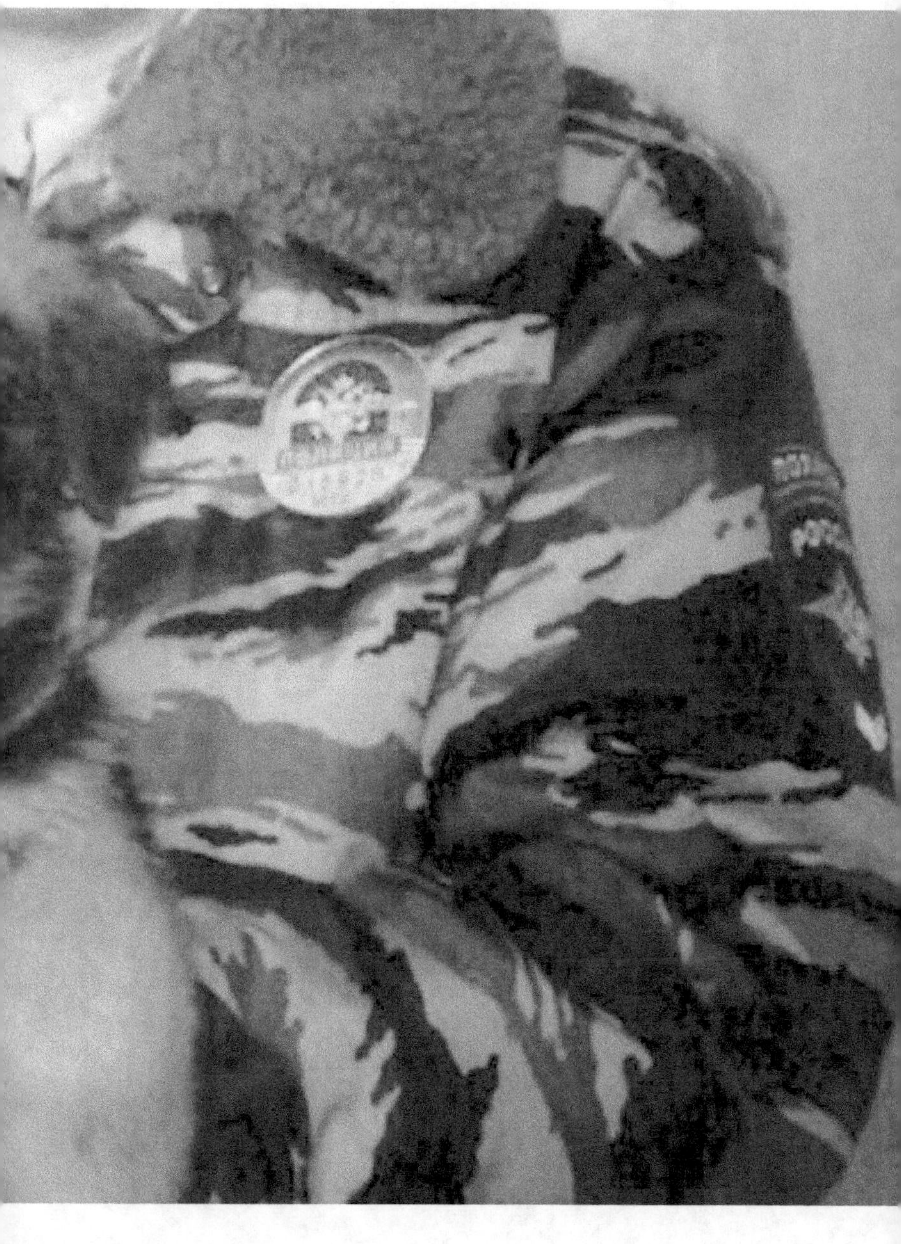

23

Who concocts the smell
of dogs which smells like
an extreme close-up
of the world oozing
in at the edges.
Full as an ice-cube is full of liquid.
I mistook it for solidity.

The world is too full of smells.
Though it's impossible
to see the top of it
they crawl between my legs
in the shimmering fuzz
on top of the plant
stickers of evenings
tongues held out
pocket-friendly air-fresheners
strikes on our nostrils.
They come at me streaming.

Why the dog? Why not
the dog? Was it only a dream
of soil heating held
and stimulated
for his unique aroma.
It's not a way in
but it places you somewhere
that smells strong
and looks strong leaving
behind us. Hi.

14

The Remaining Body of a Gage Fanfic

Uma Breakdown

Sunnydale High, High summer. A line of sand on the horizon, slowly bowing in the centre with clumps of grass and small insects.

A figure walks along this line, walking north along the coast, the sun setting on their left and eyes watching from under that sun and from under the water.

Back to the start. There's nothing for a long time. Before this Gage didn't exist and then Buffy Summers arrived and suddenly Gage exists, and they're a 'he' and that 'he' is part of the swim team at the highschool and on his first day in existence things are already pretty melancholy because his friend is dead, and their skin is all in a steaming pile on the beach, cut off shirt and Lollapalooza tattoo and there is a heinous stench and some screaming. Total bummer.

This was meant to be a party, beach fires and night surf and keg stands and sexy waterboarding celebrating the only good sports team in Sunnydale History having a chance at a state championship of some sort.

But instead, the beach stinks and people are screaming. This is how Gage starts. No wonder he's depressed.

That was Friday night, but that's not even the start. Gage, leaving the beach with all the foul odor and screaming suddenly remembers the first day he joined the team.

That was a nervous day.

Oh my, a slick entrance.

Waiting uneasy but bury that for now. Hands somewhere, waiting.

Just off the main street a single lane between the backs of houses, past an indoor market and opposite a pub with flags and posters hanging out over traffic if there was any. Still waiting, half in half out of the property, under the garage door. There's no pavement on this side of the street so it's either on the road or inside and uninvited. Hands somewhere, the sun comes out and with it the sweat and then it goes in and the water goes cold. Still waiting, ten minutes now since acknowledgement that says don't ask again I'm coming. Gage tries to worry less about creepyskin by tracking through the remembered sounds since arrival.

The car leaving.

Knocking on the panelling.

'are you interested in this? Do you know why you are here? Wait here.'

Running water like a pond, green and synthetic.

Playstation startup noise, blue and shiny.

Traffic from the main street hundred yards in either direction, muddy grey brown.

Finally, the coach returns, little man with a big presence. Wide trousers with tight cuffs, school shoes. Rolled up Sun on one pocket, miscellaneous shit in the other. Long arm allen key for pointing, some other shit that rattles.

'do you know why you're here?' repeated.

Gage responds, affirms.

Little head like a scone, smart little eyes. Sharp.

Gage fills the gap under those eyes, lists personal bests in 100m freestyle, history of water activity, awards, philosophy.

The eyes smile on, ask Gage their name

'Gage Petronzi'

'welcome to the swim team Gage Petronzi'

After this, there is so little time to think. Training takes up everything. Gage pulls the ugly sweater over his head, harsh against skin already sensitive from chlorine. Bleaching out the microbes and tightening the pores. He enters the lecture hall, amongst so many other male bodies in black and sand training wear. He studies the skull of the boy in front. Muscles in shoulders strong but loose from mornings massage circles with the B team. The neck shaved with an off centre angle, the 2mm stubble of hair starting from the bottom left. Passing more muscle and that place at the base of the skull, the indentation made to fit so many parts of a body.

An elbow
A wrist
A forehead
A palm
A cheekbone

Gage stares at that indentation, with its perfect diagonal bisection of dark hair over dark skin. Like a flag for a hyphenated politics.

Gage pours a glass of doped water from the jug in the armrest he shares with the next, empty, seat. He takes a drink as the lights are turned off and the speakers crackle once before the sound of a pulsing synthesiser arpeggio starts. A soft square wave repeating perfectly. He feels the first effects as the training film begins.

Over this full and satisfying sound, repeating and locking, comes the first images.

Grey bodies, flat in silhouette plunge feet first into a pool.

The camera rapidly cuts between three fixed positions. The body, mid-air, a few degrees off vertical, cuts through steam with a halo of light around it. The surface of the water cutting across the lens, immediately before curved toes break the summer face and destroy all image. Finally from deep below the surface that same break is repeated, a tiny explosion of bubbles in a green/black frame.

Over and over, different bodies, but the same solid breaking through three surfaces.

The drugs in the water have the same effect during every one of the twice daily lectures. Starting with a pleasant tingling in the outer corners of the eyes and an equally pleasant feeling in the neck that sprinkles it's light down the spine as he rubs it against the seat, settling lower in the movie theatre style seats. A voice starts speaking, explaining the origin of Terra.

98% of sunspots occur at 19.5° latitude.

Looping spouts of energy.

Forming a ball.

Spinning.

Solid surface expanding, swelling, drifting out away from the sun.

A ball, crusting over, all land and shallow seas, where marsupials could walk in any direction and eventually return to the world navel.

A smaller earth.

Tiny Terra.

And then years later an outside race upgraded the planet, adding water from their home world and DNA from their bodies.

Mistakes were made, and at a point when the visitors had cause to drop nuclear warheads on the surface of the planet, creating deserts and mutation among the population that had been spared and sent to the protection of underground caves.

And the tiny planet grew larger and from those refugees grew the human race, solid and perfect.

While this lecture continued, drugs worked their way further down Gage's spine, working and firing under his tailbone, and between his hips.

First in the sockets and the horror of overwhelming sensation as wormed and inched further details of muscle and tendon.

The drug colouring all the water in his body and stimulating nerves.

Opening up eyes closing them again.

Eyes closing, just little bit of white, the film still playing and the music repeating.

The back of the student's head, the indentation, stubble, now sweat and too much.

A hand through the gap of the itching wool, underneath, sweat repeat taste of drugged water nerve repeated pulse drifting swelling repeating out from the sun arc of light hand through gap drug rubbed up against the seat looping sweat stubble stretch muscle taste gap indentation through hand head pulse repeat dive between hips breath water lower beneath breathing sweat corner of eyes breathing repeat breathing. Hand through gap in itching wool.

The lecture continued for a few more minutes and then stopped before Gage regained focus. Others left the room, stepping over his body in the dark. Most still breathing hard, hands out steadying on anything that could be touched and was real.

The training goes well, weeks stretch out. Mornings waking up, the stink in clothes chemical and still painful to mucus membrane. The swim team as one hard bodied mass of slick muscle and lines in the water, zoning out everything else that isn't liquid and flesh.

That was a long time ago, and now Buffy Summers is here, and there is screaming and bad smells at the beach and Gage's friend is just a pile of skin it's looking more complicated than just training and massage and making out.

It is definitely more complicated. In fact, it's not as fun as it first seemed. The coach is more and more controlling and everything seems to be tainted with the chemical of failure. The swim team is constantly under watch, movement is analysed, breath, heart rate. Organs are monitored, focus groups examine the quality of shine on the swimmer's skin, impossible angles of dives are demanded by the public and all members of the team are photographed, filmed, sonographed and recorded at every moment. Being a member of the swim team is shit. Gage should know that now, as the star none are more under scrutiny than him. But he doesn't know, he's been soaking in chemicals and focused the stare at himself with such intensity that everything's about that.

The only thing to hate, the coach says, is failure. And then the coach calls Gage a failure.

Gage keeps moving, keeps training, but that doesn't diminish the self-loathing.

It can push it away, when you keep moving things go numb and fall away. Limbs, Skin, lungs, liver, DNA and all your left with his pumping plasma. Just the lymph nodes being worked by movement.

Training provides an immediate release, but then the effects come back harder. Depression, fractures, all the signs of abuse. A normal life is becoming impossible. A night out, a kiss and then the other person is spitting in disgust and leaving Gage broken and left in the alley behind the club to be walked home by none other than Buffy Summers. What a total failure.

The only way to cope is more training.

More input, more output, more motion.

Just that base system, water and bodies.

And then even that starts to go wrong.

Gage's body starts to ache, and someone peed in the pool and the team had to keep practicing in it anyway.

Working on breathing technique in Johnathan Levinson's piss.

Every bone hurting and skin itching and flaking and swallowing is so difficult with a swollen neck and cramping muscles one after the other and this heinous stink following you around, being dragged behind and everyone looking even here in the locker room.

Gage is just staring at his unlaced shoes on his feet, sitting on the wet bench in a highschool somehow open late into the night.

He stares at the shoes, the laces hanging, pale off white, dirty. Wet.

His whole body aches, and feels heavy. Same as every other day, and same as every other day he tries to avoid pauses like this, don't look just keep moving.

The pauses takes hold and stretches out.

He looks in the mirror in front of him. A full length mirror between every 5 grey painted lockers. His skin hangs, pale.

The skin feels heavy, hangs, still wet. Aches.

Hunched forward, arms still hanging toward unlaced shoes he sees the hanging flesh which covers his major organs. The bulge over his liver and intestine. Hanging, stretches out. Aches. Pale grey to off white in the mirror.

The flesh is heavy, holds, until it doesn't.

Wet, heavy, dirty, it hangs lower and lower.

Aching, a slow tear, and the bulges is hanging toward unlaced shoes.

All Gage can feel is the ache and the stink in the air as the broad heavy fold of organ covering flesh hangs and drops next to his shoes, and the water pooled around him mixed with Jonathan's pee and now some blood and other fluids.

In the mirror, in utter horror stares at what is underneath that fallen torn off white bulge and as the sulfurous smell of rotting fish and seaweed rolls into his lungs and gags and his eyes fill with water and drool hangs down from his open mouth.

Gage looks up, an unable to feel surprised at a figure standing by the mirror looking at him now. He didn't hear them enter and now in the mirror can seeing the hanging remains of milky gristle from ears translucent hanging down as hunched rolling forward he passes out what's left wet hard after the fall bang on dirty tiles under grey painted lockers.

There's nothing for a long time, and then there's water.

Black, but wet, felt more than anything. Small splashes close up, bigger ones further away.

There's nothing for a long time again.

Now there's vibrations, feelings on skin, proprioceptive extension. There's skin, then there's more skin further out. All of this starts realise that it's Gage.

This Gage realises that there is not just black, but grey and white, and blue, and green and red. The water is cool. Other figures bob about around. That skin that is further out, that space that is full and still permeable can feel. The figures move their bodies and through and Gage feels it. The bodies are touching, while meters apart. If Gage concentrates they call feel all the bobbing bodies, movements.

The bodies in the water look at them. Look at Gage.

They move in the water and Gage feels it. On skin, on muscle wet. A tingle on nerves that could be inside or outside the body and at this point on it does not matter which. Toes curl, solid pressure, holding different parts of this body. Of these bodies together. Like a dance, tension and eased pressure. The boundaries of each are overlapped and would be confusing if it it didn't feel like this and so good.

The boundaries between the bodies of the bobbing figures bisect through the group at multiple layers of sensation. All of them felt.

Gage looks at the bobbing figures which are just like them. Made for the water, organs that work with the sea, that connect. Lines of muscle that fit waves. Black green red surface that reflects the ocean and the sun that's setting. Gage looks up with the last of that red light and sees the figure disappear along the line of sand dunes, the coach out of a job with no one to train. The swim team moves together on a dance in the tide and the sun completely sets over Sunnydale.

15

Kathy's Body

Linda Stupart

Kathy Acker's body is small, but also very strong. Kathy Acker's hair is cut short in a signature buzzcut. Kathy Acker's hair has grown long down to her shoulders and that makes her almost unrecognisable. Kathy Acker has perfectly symmetrical ears, which stick out slightly and which point in a neat diagonal downwards. Kathy Acker's face is the kind of face you could draw diagrams on to demonstrate how to draw faces correctly and in proportion. Kathy Acker's lips are perfect red and Kathy Acker's eyebrows are in a perfect rounded arch as if they are the edges of a fingernail but drawn with goose down. I'm sorry to be such a lesbian about it, but Kathy Acker's fingers are perfectly long and tapered towards the end and her wrists are so delicate it is as if they could break at any moment if you touched them.

Kathy Acker's body is dominated by mastectomy scars worn under a leather biker jacket. Kathy Acker's chest is flat and pale like a teenage boy's and there is a large tattoo on her shoulder. Kathy Acker's breasts are pert even under an oversized loose-knit jersey. Kathy Acker's breasts are in her hands and she is biting on their nipples

Kathy Acker's eyes are in black and white and could be any colour. Kathy Acker's eyes are white tinged with red and they are hungry. Kathy Acker's left ear has three small holes in the earlobe and these are now slightly distended and empty. Kathy Acker no longer has cancer because she is dead.

The muscles on her arms bulge into rigid tumours on her shoulders and her shoulders are the shoulders of some mythical chimera and there is a small rounded hollow just inside of her shoulder blades and this would be mirrored at the point of her collarbone and I would trace my tongue along her edges. Kathy Aker's mouth is the shape and the weight of the god of desire's double curved bow and her cunt is the manifestation of the need to be loved and to be fucked. Kathy Acker's lips are slowly rotting.

Kathy has hard breasts and nipples and her firm hard naked back muscles ripple as I hold her right. There is no doubt in my mind, as I run my hands slowly over her muscular back, that I am holding a very strong vibrant woman. She has jagged scars that run along the space where she used have a perfect swollen mound of fat and I say hey baby and I line up the scar running along my chest with hers.

Kathy's body is rapidly broken down by insects and animals, including bluebottles and carrion fly maggots, beetles, ants and wasps. Her body can become a moving mass of maggots within days, even hours in hot climates. Her maggots run along my chest through hers.

Slowly, I run my hand down over her hard stomach, feeling the ripples of her hard, six-pack, abdominal muscles. I could have sworn that I could actually feel her strength and vitality pulsing thorough her muscular body as I touched her. I could feel the striations of her individual hard thigh muscles as I ran my fingers over her legs. Moving very slowly, I gently ran my hand over the smooth crotch of her white panties. Kathy's body is soft as if your fingers could just slip inside of it and break right through the skin.

I took her panties off and we were both completely naked. My pale fat body spilling over the sheets compared to her compact muscle bound fortress. I saw her big thick legs and ass. They were so big compared to the rest of her body that they had the shape of a horse ass.

Kathy's skin looks a blue green colour underneath a tattoo of a tiger holding a rose in its mouth on her bicep. Kathy's face is all fucked up. One of her eyes is dangling on her cheek. She has about five broken teeth in her mouth and blood is dripping out of it and running rivulets down her breast. She has big open sores all over her body and yellow puss is seeping out. Worms and maggots are coming out of the scar at her chest. Her penis is hard but the flesh is torn all over it. Kathy Acker's body is being eaten by a malignant mass less than five centimeters in diameter. With blood dripping from her mouth dripping onto my neck and her eyeball dangling down and bumping against my cheek and nose, I thought I was going insane.

Kathy Acker's eyes are brown and large and rounder than eyes are usually. Her nose is also rounded, but it is slightly bigger than mine. Kathy has a labia piercing that sometimes makes her cum in public.

Thick straps were placed around my arms and legs, then buckled tightly. I remember asking, "Why are you doing this?"

"Because we don't want you to harm yourself."

After sexual mutilation by a surgeon, Kathy's body shrunk even more.

"Unlike most medical stories, all the horror in this one occurs in its beginning."

Kathy Acker's cock is dripping with your cum
Kathy Acker's cock is in her mouth
Kathy Acker's mouth is in your mouth
Kathy Acker's tongue twists round your tongue
Kathy Acker's cock is in your cunt

Kathy Acker's cunt is in your cunt
Kathy Acker's arms around your neck
Kathy Acker's body beneath your body
Kathy Acker's teeth bite into your head
Kathy Acker's mouth around your insides
Kathy Acker's body around your body
Kathy Acker's breath exhales your flesh
Kathy Acker's body spits out your death.

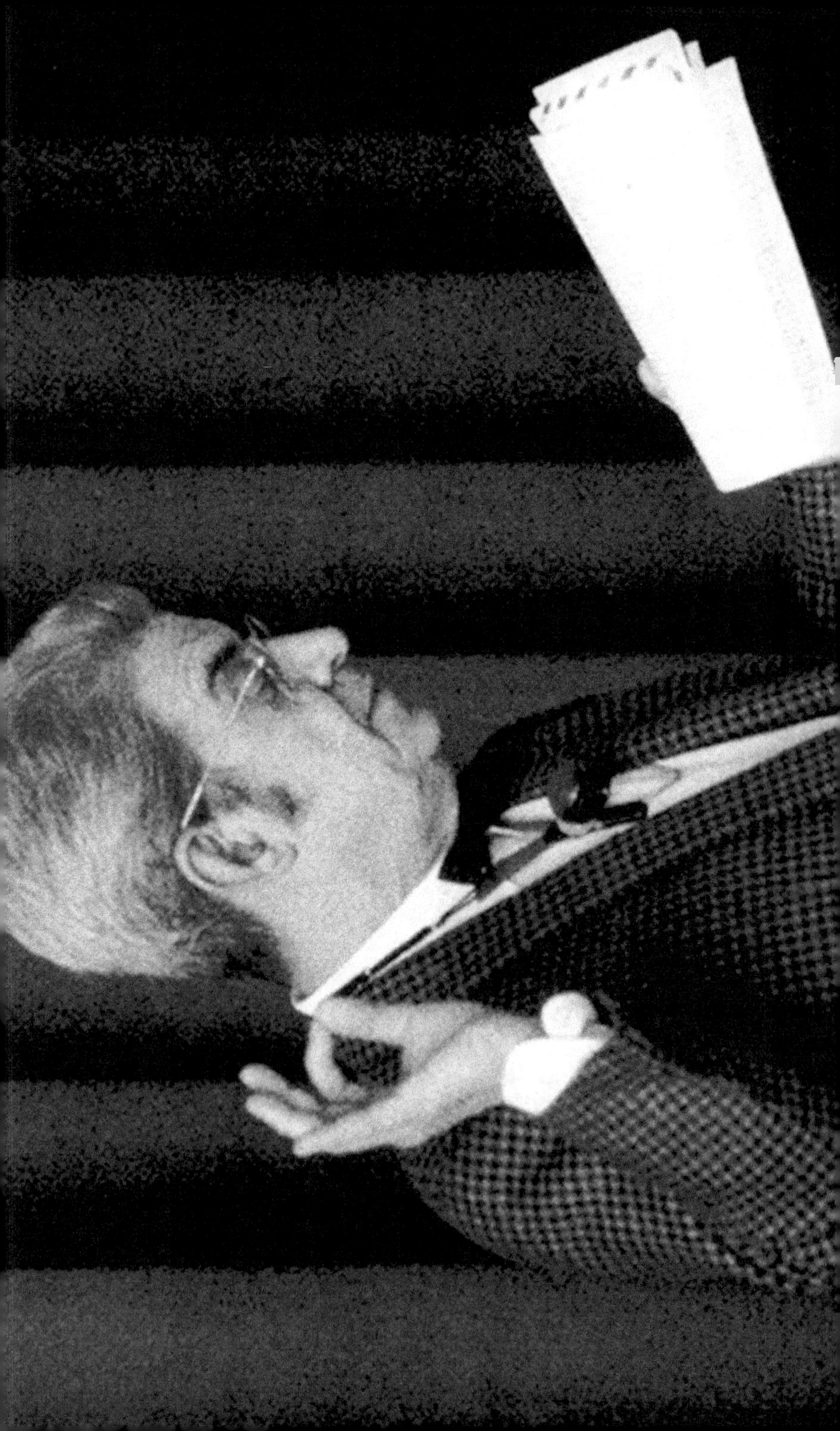

16

Envois

Sharon Kivland

I

I refuse any system. I uncover a thought in motion. I call it the dialectic. My task is to reintroduce the register of meaning. I do my dissecting with concepts, not with a knife. The man speaking to you is a man like any other — I make use of the wrong language. I allow the other to bring his language in line with mine. I think of what goes through his head when I speak to him. My ideal is *not* the absence of passion.

II

I am describing things the way they are today. I am not in a position to say more about this for the moment. What am I going to say now? I would say — when all is said and done — it is less a matter of remembering than rewriting history. I tell you what there is. I could counterpose completely different conceptions of the experience. I am certainly not the only one to have asked myself the question — I say it is a slip of the pen.

I would like to give you a still clearer sense. I would say that our actual behaviour is far from the account we give of it. I am only opening up the question. I am referring to the concrete system which doesn't have to be already spelled out for it to be there. I think I have opened up the question sufficiently for you now to see the point of what we can do together.

I am not sure if this is the exact wording, but it is very striking. I would almost say that it is a notion with retroactive effect. I portrayed for you the sum of silence after which another speech again makes its appearance. What do I want?—if not to get out of this genuine impasse. You will see that I push what I say quite far.

I am only repeating what can be found. I believe that what has happened there is a very significant failure. I believe that one must be extremely careful here. When I talk, it's so as to venture into it with unqualified analytic prudence. I think that's... It doesn't seem to me to arise out of the same cupido, if not of the same libido. I always have reservations about lots of things which aren't specified. I will try to show you in what way the danger emerges. I am not putting your opinions on trial.

III

I think I am being accurate in calling this style inquisitorial. I was about to say the trial of psychological strength. I will try to show you. When I say projection, I am not saying erroneous projection. Let there be no mistake about what I am explaining to you. Before I became an analyst, I had—thanks to what little psychological gifts I had—taken a formula as the principle of the little compass with which I appraised some situations. I was quite happy to say to myself—*Feelings are always reciprocated.* As soon as you put two subjects together—I say two, not three—feelings are always reciprocated. In fact, you need more than that, and I hope to be able to prove it to you. But I am only opening up the problem today.

It is late. Which will not allow us to go as far as I would have liked. Nevertheless, I would like to give you some sense of where we're heading. I have shown you the risks; I think it necessary to lay down some guidelines. I am pointing this out to you. I am not going to tell you the conclusion. I don't think I am being unfaithful. I would like to offer a certain number of basic concepts. I am therefore going to take an example which will make you understand clearly the questions raised by recognition, and which will keep you from drowning. I am going to tell you a little story.

I wake up in the morning with my curtain, like Semiramis, and I open one eye. I don't see this curtain every morning because it's the curtain of my house in the country, where I go only every week or so, and among the lines fomented by the fringe of the curtain I notice, once again — I say once again, I have only ever seen it once like that in the past — the silhouette of a face, all at once, sharp-edged, caricatured and old-fashioned, which for me is like the face of an eighteenth-century marquis. I can say that the curtain hasn't moved an inch since precisely eight days before. A week ago, on waking up, I had seen the same thing. I had, of course, forgotten it. If I didn't have a certain number of fantasies on what the profile represents, I wouldn't have recognised it in the fringe of my curtain.

Have you got hold of the implication of what I am saying to you? You will see that I am bringing the question to bear at the point where the re-lived is at its most ambiguous. That's where we'll start off again next time.

IV

I want to lead you to one of those points that offers perspective. I gave you advance notice. I am going to try to keep to my promise. I warn you. I am aware all of a sudden of the fact of your presence. I want to put this sharply focussed phenomenon before you. I want to stay for a moment. The little note appended to the passage that I read to you is important. I bring it up solely as an aid. I'd say it is a feeling we are always trying to efface from life. It isn't a feeling that we have all the time. I think it is something we cannot dwell upon for too long.

I am just following. It's the centre of attraction, I'd say that that is the very essence. I'll leave the theme hanging. One must play dumb each time. That's exactly what I've been telling you — there is nothing left of the dream. God knows that I have learnt to realise that desire slips runs away, appearing and disappearing before my eyes. And whose desire, anyway?

I would like to use some other examples. This is what I have been wanting to get at with these examples. Hooking onto the other is not alien. A little further and it will be seduction.

V

I showed you. I have shown you. I made you realise. I will probably not have the opportunity to return to these questions again. Our experience is not that of affective smoochy-woochy. I showed myself to be extremely guarded. I use much more clumsy expressions quite on purpose. This only opens up new problems for us.

VI

I intend to draw you into the area marked out. We have to get it moving. What I am saying to you is related to what I pointed out. The assumption of sex is decided.

VII

It wasn't without some preconceived plan. I would go as far to say that it is on the basis of a kind of refusal of understanding that we push the door open to understanding. It isn't enough for it to seem to hang together. Obviously it hangs together within the framework of pat phrases we've grown used to instinctual maturation, primitive aggressive instinct, oral, anal sadism, etc. I have taught you to identify the symbolic with language. I have concocted a little model for you. So let us rejoice. I am sorry. This little experiment pleased me. It would be fun—we'll discuss that some other day.

It isn't language I'm covertly slipping in. You will see it in the spectacular demonstration of what I am always giving to you. How can I put this in yet another way? I only wanted to introduce a bouquet. It would be worth your while to ponder the questions, to get a little feel for the schema so you could see for yourself what use you could put it to.

VIII

It is not surprising that it should be here and now that we are led. I don't think I am pushing it. We tried to define resistance within its own field. You will be well aware of the great distance that separates … that will take us to the heart of the notion. What questions do you still want to raise? I think that one can't say any more about it.

IX

That's where the opacity begins. To expect an explanation, you'll perhaps tell me, is to expect too much, to manifest too great a thirst. Several hard-headed characters would perhaps like to impose a damper on us at this point. One of the important questions is to know what is the connection between the bonds of transference and the characteristics of the love relation. We know all that. I am not taking about the course of action we sometimes undertake. It seems that there is some mysterious resistance at work, acting so to keep the question in darkness. It exerts some sort of repulsion. We are not dealing with love in the guise of Eros, but of passionate love, as a sort of psychological catastrophe. That is what is precisely at issue — what is this love?

Well, for us, what we have to locate is the structure which articulates the narcissistic relation, the function of love in its widest sense. There is more than one way to help you find your sense of direction in the midst of all the ambiguities which, as I think you have become aware, make their appearance again and again. I hope to teach you new categories. I am aiming at progress in understanding. I have my limits. I will teach you. I am going to show you. Today is only a curtain-raiser. But when it comes to matters as important as these, you can't raise the curtain too slowly. It will give you a little time to turn things over in your mind.

X

Can one say yes or no, when one is the shadow of the other? Let me clarify this. It isn't the existence of the sexual partner, the particularity of one individual, but something which has an extremely intimate relation with what I have been calling a type, namely an image. You do know, don't you, that step by step, I want to take you somewhere. Let's go back to where we first left off. And if I'm giving in on that, it's because there's a reason I'm giving in. I've been trying to explain to you for years. I'm quite happy with that. You're right in thinking it's not for the fun of it that I've made up these delightful constructions. I know not what vague fusion, or communion between genitality and the constitution of the real is recommended. It's either one or the other. We'll try to go one step further next time.

XI

I am trying to use simple terms to guide your thinking. I would like … perhaps I won't do it, I don't know. Genital love—is it a natural process? What is the point? It is through the exchange of symbols that we locate our different selves in relation to one another. We have a certain symbolic relation, which is complex. What else are we talking about when we refer to an oral, anal, genital reality? What is my desire? Love reopens the door to perfection. Next time we must clarify why this attachment is fundamentally fatal. That's what love is. It's one's own ego one loves in love. It's not every day that you come upon something that is constructed so as to give you the image of your own desire. I see that the clock ticks on.

XII

I'm beginning to slip into abstraction. You know what a delicate matter it is. There's a radical difference between the satisfaction of a desire and the pursuit of the fulfilment of desire. It's the distinction between our consciousness and our body. We recognise ourselves as body… the body as fragmented desire seeking itself out. In a moment, if you want, we'll go further. We are completely agreed that love is a form of suicide. I see that I haven't shown you enough petticoat, since you've seen the frills but not how they're tied on. If we didn't have to sort it out, we wouldn't need to be here. And that would be a great pity. Do you grasp the mechanism here? I am happy enough to use the term. This desire, we find it or we don't find it. I want to take up this point again, and at length, even if that means breaking off in the middle today. I know that I am saying these words quickly, but I will go over them again more slowly. I cannot tell you why just now. I can't satisfy you today. If you think you have understood, you are bound to be wrong. Let's leave it there for today.

XIII

I've led you here step by step. I'm putting things very crudely. I could put them in more sophisticated, philosophical language, but I want to make you see them clearly. Careful. We've already gone over these steps together. I beg you not to be too hasty. We operate as if all that goes without saying. It's a long way from what we really think. See=saw. Before desire learns to recognise itself… let us now say that word. Each time we get close, the most radical aggression arises … this all-consuming, uncontrollable jealousy. The perpetual reversion of desire to form and of form to desire… we must really understand that this game is an all-consuming one. The masochistic outcome — I never fold when raised. I am trying to respond. This seems foolish, and to go without saying. But you still have to say it and reflect on it. We still haven't got as far as I had hoped. Perhaps I am going a bit too quickly. Bear this in mind, that desire is only ever reintegrated in a verbal form. Here we find an essentially ambiguous relationship. Next time…

XIV

As I said to you, it doesn't stop there. Here we have a destructive and fatal relation. Are you satisfied, however? It seems to me that we got further last time. Desire is realised in the other, as you put it. It enters into the symbolic relation of *I* and *you*. I talked about the *fort* and *da* with you. I've repeated this time and again. All I need to do is talk about it. We must never lose sight of it. You think it's a bit much to call it the grand X? I would have no difficulty in showing you…. What is it, this supposedly accomplished genital love? If you found this too difficult… I left open the question. And we do everything. One lets go of a certain number of the moorings of speech. We are forced to see that this alone introduces a certain uncoupling. I have talked about small oscillations. I don't need to enlarge on what makes up their smallness right now. Clearly there is some braking, several occasions when things grind to a halt. Being in love happens in an entirely different way. It doesn't just happen with any partner or with just any image. I am grateful. Don't you have the feeling that this is an extremely unsatisfying game, a Utopian ideal? — which something in us is bound to be disappointed by. It is not a question of the satisfaction of desire. We will leave it there for today. I chose to climb the mountain. But let us leave matters there.

XV

I find it satisfying. The point is to bring it to its completion. That is the fertile moment. It is neither around, not roundabout, neither before, nor after, but at the exact moment when what is close to bursting open…. The copulatory position could only be restored. Let us get back to the essentials. I cannot tell you the whole story. Aren't you amazed? I will not leave it there. Are you with me? I hope this is sufficient indication of direction I am taking. I haven't exhausted it. I am going to try to get you to understand. That is pushing things very far. You are going to think that I am overstepping the limits. It is always a delicate matter. We are no way relieved of the problems raised by the relations of desire. That is what we just now encountered. Where should this adjournment come to a stop? That is where I will leave you today.

XVI

Do let us try to get something out of it. Everything which is good for me is right for you. It is not for nothing that the real is always in the background. It is late now. Is it emotions that are transferred? Till next Wednesday.

XVII

Let us go straight to the knot. I cannot linger over this. If there exists a tendency towards perfect satisfaction, in all strictness exactly the same has to hold for the other side. There is a direct stitching together of desires which dovetail together, bind together. There's no getting away from it. There will just have to be an object to satisfy and saturate it. The satisfaction of the one, I won't say is concerned for the satisfaction of the other, but is saturated in this satisfaction. That is incredible. When we arrive at the level of the genital relation, there is no way of making it develop any further. You must extricate yourself from this fascination to fall on your feet again, that is what I am trying to remind you of now. Let us leave to one side the voyeuristic and exhibitionistic relations — that is too easy to prove. Let us take the sadistic relation… playing the waiting game, playing on the fear of the other, with pressure, with threat, keeping to the forms, more or less secret. One can go further. Have I wrapped things up enough to be able to leave you at this point? That doesn't mean there won't be a sequel. I will prove it to you next time.

XVII

I think you have understood what blind alleys this leads one into. I gave you an introduction to the experience of sadism, which I took to be elective in revealing this dimension to you. I pointed out that, in the gaze of the being I torment, I have to sustain my desire with an act of defiance, a challenge at every instant. If it does not arise above the situation, if it is not glorious, desire sinks into shame. Perversion as I have delineated it for you can only be sustained within a precarious status. It is always fragile, at the mercy of an inversion, a subversion. Perversion is an experience which allows us to enter more deeply into what one can call, in the full sense, the human passion. It becomes a profound experience. Either desire is extinguished, or the object disappears. That is why, at every turn, I take my bearings from the master-slave dialectic. The term doesn't frighten me. I won't push this today. We come upon the famous problem of two bodies. We can stop for a moment. And we make strenuous efforts. What does that imply? I have already talked about the state of narcissistic eruption in one of our meetings.

XIX

I am exceedingly happy. It is me, my being, my avowal, my invocation. Once more, I will try to make you see it. Let us try to be a little bit coherent. What I am saying is downright simple-minded. But it is only by making the structure a bit more explicit, and in saying simple things, that we will learn to spell out in words of one syllable the elements of the situation in which we act. We are talking about things, and not about some eternally unidentifiable I know not what. We find ourselves at the heart of the problem. It is true, and it isn't. There is nothing present, nothing emotional, nothing real in this situation. None of this is easy. Are you with me? There are essential relations which no discourse can express adequately. On this note I will leave you today.

XX

You do realise, don't you, the extent to which we are at the heart of what I have been trying to explain to you? Either we already know the truth in question, or we do not know it.

XXI

Today your fidelity, up to now unfailing, is flagging somewhat. And at the end of the race, it is I who will have had you. We have arrived at the central point. Either you've got it or you haven't. I wish only to open a small door for you, whose threshold we will someday cross. We have seen that deception can only be sustained as a function of the truth. Is it unthinkable that it might come about? You can call this upheaval what you will. Our abortive actions are actions which succeed, those of our words which come to grief are those which own up. These acts, these words reveal a truth from behind. Reality is what makes it so that when I am here, you, my dear lady, cannot be in the same place. Haven't I put you in a good enough position?

XXII

I am delighted by your question. There are profound reasons why you are left craving for more. What, in short, are you still craving for? If you are with me, we will be able to go a long way. The question is not so much one of knowing up to what point one should go, the question is more one of knowing if one will be followed. The position we are in is different, more difficult. Love is distinct from desire. Now learn to distinguish love as an imaginary passion. With hate, it is the same thing. Don't get me wrong. In speaking about love and hate to you, I am showing you paths for the realisation of being. I beseech you. Where does this take us? You have to wait. You have to wait as long as it takes.

AFTERWORD

I started to write thinking about Lacan's hair, having read an interview with his hairdresser (which may have been invented—I did not ascertain). This made me think, of course, about Derrida's hair, a mane opposed to *en brosse.* However, I was distracted by Derrida's *envois* in *The Post Card,* the sendings to an unnamed beloved (whom one may perfectly well name now as Sylviane Agacinski). This led me (a roundabout and illogical route) to an early seminar of Lacan, his teaching on the training programme of the Société Française de Psychanalyse, following Freud's papers on technique, Lacan's insistence on a return to Freud. This year-long seminar addresses resistance, narcissism, the imaginary, repression, desire, perversion, the creative function of speech.... I have in my careful re-reading and re-writing removed all of *that,* all that psychoanalytic theory, while retaining Lacan's words and his alone (I have added nothing, I avow) as a series of twenty-two love letters, envois addressed to a beloved, unnamed (a 'dear lady'), following the course of a love affair. And yet, well, and yet, all *that* remains as my master breaks the silence.

17

Wilhelm Reich

Harman Bains

Wilhelm Reich (1897–1957), the famed Austrian psychoanalyst, was renowned for developing methods to harness the power of pleasure. Intent on researching the power of pleasure for the advancement and well-being of the human body, Reich found himself preoccupied with the functionality of sexual satisfaction.

Pain as a condition of sexual pleasure is a well-documented phenomena; bodies carousing in limitations opposed by facets of inhibition no longer impart fear into the conventional. Sexual pleasure as a cure for pain is a relatively unknown condition. Often considered as a short-lived chemical experience pleasure derived from sexual interaction to oneself or another promotes a sense of a calm and well-being through an instant but soon diminishing release of oxytocin.

The prospects of cure and the success of the cure are directly dependent upon the possibility of establishing the capacity for full genital gratification.

THE SOURCE

galvanised steel
steel wool
fibreglass
steel wool
fibreglass
steel wool
fibreglass
wood frame
soundboard

On entering a large hollow capacitor composed of alternate layers of insulators and conductors, the resting biological state of the human body manifests to a parasympathetic state, otherwise referred to as a 'pleasure reaction'. A single seat housed inside an unassuming rectangular box harnesses energy that directly charges the bioelectric circuits of the human body. Named by Wilhelm Reich, the Orgone Accumulator was created to channel this energy and was observed by Reich to have a direct effect onto the human biological system, directly expressed in the emotion and sexual function of the user. A persons' overall volatility and aliveness was a function of human atmospheric organ charge impulsation — which Reich titled 'the bioelectrical investigation of sexuality and anxiety'. This simple enclosure ensured a high charge of energy to collect inside its walls and pass freely through the body within. The organic layer attracted and held an energy originating from the atmosphere. The metallic layer attracted then simultaneously repelled the life energy in both directions. The organic layer than re-passed the life energy back to the metallic later and the metallic layer begins to radiate the life energy to the inside where it remained. A one-way flow was set up from the outside layer to the user, similar to a capacitor or diode. A feedback effect was created as the person inside reflected their own living energy resulting in the full charging of the human body.

The orgone charge of the tissues was a fundamental component of the immune system and sexuality. In opposition to anxiety or danger impulses, pupils dilated in response to the heightened pleasure environment. Water glands, including salivary and sweat, exhibited their output by celebrating secretion; the dominant heart muscle demonstrated its response by slowing its pulse and the plentiful piloerector muscles relaxed to display un-bristled smooth skin. Genitals demonstrated their induction of pleasure, the male penis, once aroused, would enlarge from its flaccid state, whereas the female vagina would begin to secrete fluid from its original dry state. *There is only one thing wrong with the neurotic patients: the lack of full and repeated sexual satisfaction.*

Individually self-regulated sexual existence relies upon orgasms as a gateway to health and freedom. This release of energy by the body, once inside, provided evidence that the Freudian Libido was in fact a real energy discharged during emotional expression and sexual orgasm. Punishment manifested through parental or social hegemony, against youthful expression of emotion, or sexuality turned to internalised repression. This repression was manifested by the literal tightening of ones muscles, a binding force of conflict and tension evidenced by the formation of a neuro-muscular armouring that blocked the capacity for pleasure and happiness, including sexual excitation. Reich considered the analogy of the female egg that divides when internal pressure and surface tension reach a certain level. Since the human organism cannot do this, it can only be masochistic, pleading to an orgiastic discharge of pent-up energy. The orgasmic energy appeared to move in two directions out of the self, towards the world.

The discovery of the life energy would have been accomplished long ago, had this 'I don't want it, I fear it, I loathe it, I'll kill it, I'll flatten it out, I won't let it exist live, or exist'. If that had not been in their structures, not in their desires, not in their positive conscious wishes. They cannot tolerate it and they fear it. They fear it by way of structure. Their tissues, their blood cannot stretch out, cannot take it, evades it—avoids it and loathes it.

Orgasmic potency is the capacity for sexual surrender without any reservations, the capacity for complete discharge of all dammed-up sexual excitation through involuntary, pleasurable convulsions of the body.

THE PLEASURE

aluminium frame
tempered glass
sliding door mechanism
chrome
brushed nickel
swivel connection
anti lime-scale nozzle
lead pipes
viaduct system

An unremarkable set of coincidences allowed for the discovery of a variable pressure showerhead to induce orgasms. The wonderment of this breakthrough instructs the vaginal glands to manage copious amount of secretion in an already wet environment. The constant supply of water and slight changes to temperature during high pressure allows for hands free masturbation. The jet stream will hit the hood of the clitoris and inner labia but fail to penetrate the vestibule of the mouth of the vagina. Without vaginal invasion the orgasm can induce feelings of emptiness, but a prolonged feeling of fullness to the vulva continues to warm and plump.

Curiosity is a fundamental motivation for the exploration of body parts. The location of ones genitalia, the differences in function and use for the opposite sexes enlightens a sense of belonging to one's body. The deterrence of such curiosity can cause a hyper state of sexuality that if not acted upon and can impose a trauma to the body. The understanding of Reich's objective for a full simulation of mind and body for the possibility of pleasurable stimulation, is to access a higher state of oneself.

If not too un-slightly an orgasm can be achieved in the most ordinary of environment, a re-purposed domestic space that can be used comfortably and repeatedly for orgasmic pleasure can in effect achieve a loosening of body armor in similar to Reich's orgone accumulator. The original was not specially designed to house spontaneous orgasm nor did most achieve this, but a heightened state of pleasure was foreseeable. A fit for purpose accumulator depending on levels of genital stimulation can achieve higher amounts of orgasmic fulfillment, thus disarmoring one's body.

Two glass panels held together by an aluminum frame were positioned in the corner of the room. One point five meters in length, the focal showerhead was mounted on the tiled wall to the left. On entering, the human body would gravitate towards the right panel until the correct water temperature was in full flow. Aforementioned piloerector muscles constrict to preserve body heat abruptly exiting the fleshy mass. A temperature of forty degrees is the common denominator for a successful cleanse. Forty-five degrees is preferential. A removable showerhead with varying pressure outputs is essential for sustained pleasure. On wetting the body a suitable position is assumed directly below the flow, the rounded head, an arms width away. The removal of showerhead from its bracket begins the process of pleasure. The turning of the pressure clockwise ensures that a strong force of current is maintained. A seated pose, though optional, can be adopted to ensure ease to the spreading of legs. The nozzle points directly at the hood of the clitoris. On impact the labia will be forced apart, the discomfort at first will ease and a slight numbing sensation will assist in the continued use of high pressure to the genitalia. As if by chance the very manufacturing of this object is suited to both the grip and the vagina of the beholder.

Legs parted, the tendons located in either thigh are pulled tightly as the coccyx is adjusted to avoid any discomfort from the hard wet floor. One arm lay beside the angled body, the other rose above stretched legs — the chrome head reflecting a thirsty labia. The force of the jets leaping from the cunt to the glass sliding door, a vigorous tapping the glass panel, small droplets forming on the aluminum frame. As the body adjusts to the constant pounding a slow surge of pleasure will began to ooze out from the drenched pink skin, a thicker texture effortlessly combining with the water. A slight elevation in the pelvis ensures that the pressure caresses the most outward flesh. The pulsating jets, if prepared correctly, can enable a sustained and powerful orgasm. The reaching of the climax will begin to transform the lower abdomen as it tenses, the sensation will travel through to the perineum allowing the bodily form to change shape uncontrollably; violent spasms wrecking form, an effort to maintain control whilst the body contorts through the vicious pleasure tremors, the jets become a force too hard for the now tenderized flesh — the swivel connection reversed until normal pressure resumed. Standing upright a gentle hand against the lower abdomen will ease discomfort and all for water stored in the vestibule to be released. The tender pink. The combination of liquids; dense and solvent.

THE PAIN

Composite construction
2mm CR4 double skin steel plate wrapped and fully welded door leaf
internal steel structural core matrix with internal thermal / acoustic insulation Optional viewing windows
food hatch
shackle hatch
inundation points
anti barricade facility

'Paranoia manifested by delusions of grandiosity and persecution and ideas of reference.'

On being convinced the scientific world would recognize the value of his work and appreciate the great benefit of orgone energy, Wilhelm Reich encouraged a great pain onto his body. In February 1954, an injunction was issued forbidding the interstate shipment of orgone accumulators' also denying the existence of orgone energy and thus sabotaging his work and legacy. Refusing to abide by the terms of the injunction, Reich argued the legal court could not evaluate his scientific work, thus summoned to trial and arrested in May 1956. Awaiting trial, Reich's published journals, papers and publications were burnt and many accumulators axed to oblivion. In March 1957, Reich was imprisoned.

Prolonged stress imbalances the central nervous system. When these emotion sensors of the brain activates its sympathetic nervous system, but is uncompensated by the parasympathetic nervous system, a rush of adrenalin is released into the body, over time and if the stress is constant it can cause myocardial cells to break down, thus affecting the blood flow to the heart muscle. Total deprivation results in an area of infarction, causing vital cells to die and thus resulting in the tissues becoming necrotic. The most outstanding symptom of acute myocardial infarction is a sudden painful sensation of pressure in the chest, occasionally radiating to the arms, throat and back and persisting for a number hours. Pallor, profuse perspiration and signs of shock are present. Extreme apprehension and a sense of impending death are apparent.

The organization of social life determines the quantity and the quality of the equalization of tension and discharge in the psychic apparatus. If there is a lack of social possibilities for genital gratification; if the measure of unpleasurable stimuli is too great owing to distress and want, the psychic apparatus works with substitute mechanisms that seek to bring about some discharge at any cost. The results are neuroses, perversions, pathological changes of character, anti-social manifestations of genital life and, not least, work disturbances.

On the 3rd November 1957, Reich suffered a blockage in his left heart ventricle, and died in Danbury Federal Prison. A myocardial infarction of the interior wall of the left ventricle results in a secondary thrombosis conclusion of the interior-ascending branch of the left coronary artery, death imminent. Decomposition begins several minutes after death. This self-digestion is caused by the now defunct heart muscle failing to pump oxygen to vital organs and cells in the body. This deprivation increases a toxic by product of chemical reactions causing enzymes to consume the cell membrane and leak out as the cell breaks down. Body temperature begins to drop as rigor mortis begins in the eyelids, jaw and neck muscle before continuing into the limbs. Filamentous proteins actin and myosin are depleted of their energy source, unable to slide along each other they lock in place causing the muscles to become rigid and locked.

It became clear that repression of sexuality has the function of making people susceptible to exploitation and suppression.

18

The Missing Body of JT Leroy

Pil and Galia Kollectiv

Not much remains of the body of JT Leroy. To start with, it is a body first and foremost made of words. Over the course of debut novel *Sarah,* short story collection *The Heart Is Deceitful Above All Things* and the novella *Howard's End,* this body is portrayed as highly attuned to the sensual qualities of the mostly grim world it inhabits. It endures extremes of physical torture, from a disciplinarian grandfather's whipping to sexual abuse from mother Sarah's boyfriends. It registers the ultra-specific smells that pervade its low-rent environment, from the Naugahyde upholstery of car seats to the overwhelming, eye-searing odour of freshly cut ramps, a kind of wild onion native to West Virginia. The reader's ability to empathise with this damaged body—to vicariously feel the impact of the drugs, sex and violence that it is subjected to—is at the heart of the entire project. And yet for all the power of these descriptions to conjure the intensity of lived experience, the actual existence of this body has only ever been fragmentary at best, dispersed across telephone calls, emails, stand-ins and other evasive manoeuvres.

We first spoke to JT, as many had at the time, over the phone. He was charming, articulate and very sweet as he tried to help us get to grips with the mystery of how a barely educated street kid from an impoverished background might possess the literary skills in evidence in his artfully composed novel, which borrowed from the Southern legacy of writers like William Faulkner and Harry Crews, combining an ear for dialect with biblical references. JT described the biblical writing exercises assigned by his religious grandfather and his own childhood street preaching as the training ground for this ability, and whilst we remained sceptical of the autobiography, we were deeply impressed with the writing itself and stayed in touch, even asking him for a story for a publication we made later that year. Three years later, we met in a hotel lobby for a press junket on the occasion of the release Asia Argento's film of *The Heart Is Deceitful Above All Things*. Despite the reassurances of the Foyles' representative, we wrote, 'even now, having met JTLeRoy in a posh hotel in London, seen him sans wig and sunglasses, we still feel that the lucid dream of a narrative he has crafted in his three slim books is somehow more real than the man himself'.[1] He appeared very feminine, but explained that this was due to gender reassignment. More bizarrely, he did not seem to remember details from our earlier conversation and correspondence, and overall seemed a lot more withdrawn and far less able to elaborate on the ideas expressed in the writing. It turned out this was more than just a case of extreme shyness.

As is well known by now, Jeremiah 'Terminator' Leroy was the invention of Laura Albert, a middle aged New Yorker who had worked as a telephone sex operator and porn writer, whilst pursuing a musical career with her partner Geoffrey Knoop in the band Daddy Don't Go. Adept at using her verbal skills in creating fantasy narratives, she crafted the persona of the traumatised teenage sex worker whose sordid life as an Appalachian 'lot-lizard' became the subject of several books and used it to promote the writing. Using a fake Southern accent over the phone, she gained the support of established writers like Dennis Cooper and Mary Gaitskill and quickly rose to the kind of

1 Pil and Galia Kollectiv, 'King of the Street', *Plan B Magazine* 6 (June–July 2005): 86–87.

stardom that had so far eluded her but that also required in person appearances. Albert employed a series of avoidance tactics, before settling on her partner's sister, Savannah Knoop, forever in wig and dark sunglasses, as the incarnation of the author's body and posing as his friend/minder, a cockney punk rocker called Speedie:

> No one had ever met him in person, and there were starting to be rumors that he was not real, so I knew I needed to supply a body. I made a date to meet Mary [Gaitskill], and I decided to hire someone to play JT. But I didn't know anybody who matched my physical description of JT. So Geoff and I got in the car and started driving up and down Polk Street, and I saw a boy I'd never seen before. He was nineteen and he was slight, blond, blue-eyed—perfect. I said to him, You want to make fifty bucks, no sex? He said, Sure. I just told him not to talk, just say hello to a woman named Mary, get freaked out, and leave. I took him to the café. Mary Gaitskill was sitting there. The kid walked up to her, said, Hi, I'm Terminator, and he handed her some vinegar and chocolate—things I brought to give her as gifts. She said, Hi, glad to meet you, and when the kid ran off, I sat down. I was there as Speedie, and we talked.[2]

It would be easy to dismiss the hoax, as many have done, as an exercise in celebrity. Many of Leroy's initial supporters ended up disavowing any merits they originally identified in his writing once Albert's identity as the writer behind the stories was confirmed. Cooper in particular, insisted on the importance of the truth value of the story, which was odd considering the role the construction of literary fantasy takes in his own writing in relation to transgressive sex and violence:

2 Nathaniel Rich, 'Being JT Leroy', *The Paris Review* 178 (Fall 2006), http://www.theparisreview.org/miscellaneous/5664/being-jt-leroy-nathaniel-rich.

> 'He' originally seduced me and a number of other writers with his misery and horror filled autobiography and his seemingly remarkable ability to not only have survived that life but to have such a bright future ahead of 'him' due to 'his' inexplicable talent as a writer and the courage 'he' showed in using art as a weapon to face down all that abuse. All writers who believe writing is important want a reason to believe, because there aren't many reasons out there these days, and JT Leroy was a reason, a real flesh and blood, authentic reason to believe writing remained a very important medium.[3]

But why was it so important for Leroy's body to have experienced this misery and horror? Is the writing only validated by bearing testimony to this corporeal suffering? What can we learn from this broken body, scattered across texts, impersonations and media encounters?

In an interview for *The Moth,* Albert explains that 'one reason JT was so shy was because JT didn't have a body'.[4] And yet, for someone whose body was missing in action, JT had a surprisingly strong physical presence. Despite never having properly existed, JT Leroy had an ear. Speaking at the Public Theater in 2003, Winona Ryder described an improbably first meeting with JT when she saw him listening in to the opera house a decade earlier, a street kid with his ear to the wall.[5] Despite never having properly existed, JT Leroy had a disfiguring skin condition that, at least for a while prevented him from making public appearances: a photograph of George Miles, Dennis Cooper's childhood friend and muse, became another proxy.[6] Despite never

3 Dennis Cooper, 'A JT Leroy riff', *Dennis Cooper's* (blog), 28 October 2005, https://web.archive.org/web/20061027194405/http://denniscooper.blogspot.com/2005/10/jt-leroy-riff.html.

4 'Laura Albert at The Moth "My Avatar & Me"', *YouTube,* 24 November 2010, https://www.youtube.com/watch?v=oxAHHXEoHOw.

5 'Winona on JT Leroy', *YouTube,* 16 September 2011, https://www.youtube.com/watch?v=iCfMIItHhjU.

6 Stephen Beachy, 'Who Is the Real JT Leroy?: A Search for the True Identity of the Literary Hustler', *New York Magazine,* n.d., 5, http://nymag.com/nymetro/news/people/features/14718/index4.html.

having properly existed, JT Leroy had sex with Asia Argento, excusing the ace bandage covering his breasts as a post-op way of protecting privacy.[7] Despite never having properly existed, JT Leroy had a lung, a mutant part of her own body, which Albert claimed to share.[8] In several statements following the exposure of the hoax, she refers to this need for a corporeal manifestation:

> He felt very trapped in my body. For me it was a relief being able to find a body where he could rest, where he was able to move into my own body.[9]

> He wanted his own body. He so wanted to be out of me. I wanted this other child I had to be out in the world. He didn't like being inside me. He could talk such smack about me.[10]

There were parts missing:

> …in person, the body had no eyes. Behind the wig and the sunglasses was a stand-in, an avatar, an enactment, a living mask.[11]

Even more significant were the anatomical absences that photographer Mary Ellen Mark observed when she was invited to create a portrait of the author:

> Over the course of two days in April I photographed JT in Knoop's house and at various other locations. To me, it was

7 Savannah Knoop, *Girl Boy Girl: How I Became JT LeRoy* (New York: Seven Stories Press, 2008), 19.

8 Rich, 'Being JT Leroy'.

9 'Laura Albert talks with dot429', *YouTube*, 9 November 2011, https://www.youtube.com/watch?v=Tofr401Xtkc.

10 Alan Feuer, 'Writer Testifies about Source of Nom de Plume', *New York Times*, 20 June 2007, http://www.nytimes.com/2007/06/20/nyregion/20cnd-writer.html.

11 See 'Remembering Mary Ellen Mark,' *Laura Albert*, 28 May 2015, https://lauraalbert.org/remembering-mary-ellen-mark/.

> obvious right away that JT was biologically female. She didn't have an Adam's apple and she had pretty, beautiful skin.[12]

So what are we to make of this recasting of the fictionalised autobiography of JT Leroy as a work of pure fiction? Are we to disregard the author's identity altogether? Re-reading the novels with this knowledge is inevitably ironic. When Sarah says, 'most anything you want in this world is easier when you're a pretty girl',[13] it is hard not to think about the woman who authored these words, by now a bit too old to be that pretty girl, trying to pass for a boy and then casting a girl to be that boy becoming a girl. But rather than trying to rise above this information to perform some kind of abstracted reading of the text as emanating from an ethereal, universalised non-body, we would argue that there is a lot to be gained from considering it within the tradition of the extensive literature of passing. What is at stake in the strange case of JT Leroy goes beyond the ambiguous gendering of the writer's body. Many women have, of course, assumed masculine pseudonyms to facilitate a career in publishing, from George Sand to George Eliot, but in some ways Laura Albert has more in common with Boris Vian, the white Frenchman who pretended to be a black man to write a novel about a light skinned African American passing for a white man and seeking racial vengeance. Vian was spurred to write *I Spit on Your Graves* by a bet with a publisher friend that he could write a best seller in 10 days. He was revealed as the author of the controversial book when it was banned for obscenity, but in performing this double bluff, he exposed the essentialist views of race that prevailed at the time, a lethal cocktail of stereotypes from virility to violence. Whether as a side-effect of his unmasking or in keeping with his anti-essentialist views, in raising the possibility of passing and then embodying this himself, Vian

12 Diane Pernet, 'Laura Albert with Mary Ellen Mark's portrait of JT LeRoy at SF Camerawork', *A Shaded View on Fashion*, 2 June 2015, http://ashadedviewonfashion.com/blog/laura-albert-mary-ellen-marks-portrait-jt-leroy-sf-camerawork.

13 JT Leroy, *Sarah* (London: Bloomsbury, 2000), 10

questioned the mapping of race onto identity as an easy binary of white and black.

It is in comparison to Vian's project that Laura Albert's ruse is best interrogated, because JT Leroy isn't merely a (transgendered) male body that serves as a vehicle for the (still subaltern) female author. That quote from Mary Ellen Mark continues:

> She didn't look like someone from an impoverished background. She was kind of classy, educated, and smart — not a person who was a victim of real poverty. She was nice and sweet, very cooperative, and incredibly theatrical, so I played along with it.[14]

The body of JT Leroy is encoded not only through gender but also, crucially, through class: punky hairstyle and scrappy attire aside, it does not 'read' sufficiently like the body of a poor person. A closer reading of JT Leroy's writing reveals this incongruity to be the crux of the matter. Sarah in particular is dense with descriptions of gourmet food. The conceit is that the truck stop diner where the lot lizards ply their trade is staffed by a former male prostitute who had been offered a way out by his pimp if he trained as a chef and served the tricks the kind of memorable meals that would guarantee repeat visits. Bolly Boy serves flambéd pecan soufflé, Appalachian fois gras apple pie and a 'surprisingly tasty tomato and ramp sorbet with mayonnaise crème'.[15] Playing on the expectations the reader might have of a 'white trash' writer, the novel at once relies on all the stereotypes of trailer park poverty and Christian fundamentalism, while at the same time undermining these through an urbane culinary vocabulary that belies this kind of upbringing. The hyper-sensitive body of JT Leroy is primed for the most horrendous torture. We can readily accept that like his young uncle Aaron, he might be

14 Pernet, 'Laura Albert with Mary Ellen Mark's portrait of JT LeRoy at SF Camerawork'.

15 Leroy, *Sarah*, 52.

locked for hours in a punishment box, its floor covered in dried peas that will leave little deep round craters on his knees.[16] But this body is not meant to have consumed or even tasted such arcane delights as French shallots in a saffron-infused lobster-reduction sauce.

Far more interesting than the misery memoir Laura Albert worked so hard to market, the case of JT Leroy, in light of the revelation of the 'hoax', turns out to be an investigation of authenticity, so fundamental to the great American narrative. The strong need for firm and correct semiotic link between cultural narrative and corporeal carrier is nowhere more apparent than in the recent case of the Rachel Dolezal, the American activist and professor of Africana studies whose parents accused of misleadingly 'passing' as black. A tangible sense of anxiety is attached to any deviation from this semiotic function. This anxiety is not coincidental and reflects more than a racial nervousness that white America feels towards the globalised world it inhabits.

There has been much discussion in critical theory in recent years about the way in which the production of subjectivity has become a site of value extraction for post-Fordist workers. Extending beyond the creative industry, the demand to produce the self as a commodity is apparent throughout the service sector, an unending performance of the self through customer relations, social media interactions and an increasingly vague boundary between friendship and networking. Work in the west today is organised around the display or voicing of subjective, social, cognitive and linguistic skills through constant and repetitive actions: liking, sharing, posting, rating, commenting and caring and communicating in general. Since this neoliberal transformation of the social into a field of economic production is done with words, stories and opinions, one would expect a

16 JT Leroy, *The Heart is Deceitful Above All Things* (London: Bloomsbury 2001), 78.

lax attitude towards the malleability of identity. After all, it is constructed everyday through work, extracted way beyond its shell of subjective 'authenticity'. And indeed in the early days of the communication technologies that made this mode of production possible, this was sometimes celebrated as a potential form of liberation: on the internet nobody can tell if you're a dog (or, more likely, a cat). But this early attitude has changed into reactionary re-emergences of the authentic self, armed with a matching body, 'real-life' name and a corroborate-able life story. This is because, despite the infinite flexibly and expansion of neoliberal and post-Fordist work, the self is still the Achilles heel of the system. The flurry of economic activity has to be tied to an individual in order to generate value. In the same way that liquid capital is exchanged and multiplied at the speed of light only to be re-solidified in the form of property, the only possible investment of the neoliberal age, so is the incessant chatter of post-Fordist work captured in the inviolable authentic subject.

In the context of industrial labour, class distinctions were closely related to occupation and to the body: whether your collar and your face were dirty or clean determined what social group you belonged to. But with this new kind of social labour, the tools of the trade seem increasingly identical. If we are to see the self as the new factory, the place where value is created from the raw material of the human, then perhaps we might need to start looking at class as a question of our access to that means of production that is our subjectivity. Possession of the cognitive skills that enable us to consciously construct our 'selves' is not equally distributed. The ability to access education or therapy, the means to buy Adderall or retrain to attain new skills, the capacity to play with identity without violent reprecussions, these may well be the new markers of distinction.[17] In other words, the

17 The latter is neatly demonstrated in Judith Butler's essay about the film *Paris Is Burning*, where she considers the different fates of Venus Xtravaganza and Willi Ninja: '[Venus] "passes" as a light-skinned woman, but is — by virtue of a certain failure to pass completely — clearly vulnerable to homophobic violence; ultimately, her life is taken presumably by a client who, upon the

self becomes a loose fictional anchor, an investment portfolio that securitizes the value of acts of communication against a measurable and rigid 'belonging' to a particular social group.

In this respect, JT Leroy's body is not just a site of over-production that spreads across several identities and (physical and fictional) forms. The 'Other' of the elastic neoliberal subjects who remodel their bodies and minds with ease (in the gym, through drugs or through flexible international educational frameworks) is not only the immobile and inactive subject, unable to keep producing the self (because of police restrictions, border control or the inaccessibility of transformative platforms). It is also the missing body, the one that disappears without a trace in the failed crossing of the Mediterranean or the one that collapses under the burden of being a site of production. 'Natoma Street', the story that closes *The Heart Is Deceitful Above All Things* is a beautiful illustration of why Leroy's books are a powerful exploration of this theme as they fuse together the literary body as a subject and as a form. The young protagonist in the story buys a potentially life threatening sadomasochistic sexual act with no 'safe word'. Just before the narrative delves into the predictable torture scenario, it is abruptly disrupted and the reader is confronted with another, earlier, scene in which Sarah allows and even encourages a shop keeper to humiliatingly punish a younger version of our teenage protagonist. Here, the graphic lacerations are conspicuously absent from the story, more missing fragments of a missing body. This elliptical structure acts of course as a psychological explanation for why a teenage boy would seek and even pay for torture — an obvious psychoanalytical site of trauma that reverberates later in life. But it is more

discovery of what she calls her "little secret," mutilates her for having seduced him. On the other hand, Willi Ninja can pass as straight; his voguing becomes foregrounded in her video productions with Madonna et al., and he achieves post-legendary status on an international scale. There is passing and then there is passing, and it is — as we used to say — "no accident" that Willi Ninja ascends and Venus Xtravaganza dies.' Judith Butler, *Bodies That Matter: On the Discursive Limits of 'Sex'* (London: Routledge, 2011), 89.

than that. Subversively, the protagonist here wishes to disappear, to gain pleasure from the reduction of and damage to his body, to author his own torture scene. The gap between the two parts of the story doesn't really explain anything, as neither narrative has priority or more 'authentic' status. We don't even know whether the second part is a hallucination, a memory or simply another parallel short story contained within the first, and considering the magical realism that pervades Leroy's Southern Gothic fantasy, any of those is plausible. But the key difference between the two narratives is that in the first one, the character merges a little with the author by designing his own harm: casting the role of the tormentor, choosing specific devices of torture, providing whispered instructions.

That Laura Albert was able to author a fiction that seems unlikely for a real 'JT Leroy' to have written isn't merely a testament to the prejudices of the publishing industry and the reading public. It is also emblematic of the deep social gaps that run through American society. In the wake of her discovery, Albert, who was sued by the film company that had optioned Sarah for signing a contract under a false identity, attempted to claim back some of the authenticity of the story by stating that she had experienced street life and abuse. But the parts of the story that don't add up, that refuse to confirm the demand that one writes what one knows, are far more compelling in terms of their implications. Albert was able to move fluidly between genders, ages and accents, drift between hired bodies and trade in the different voices she could project, in a way that a less well-travelled Appalachian transgendered prostitute might have struggled to do. But in doing so, she has forced the question of the role authenticity plays in the construction of human capital. What is this thing we are supposedly born with, but that we are then also meant to invest in for meritocratic gains? If we are the owners of our human capital, that quality we are meant to promote and monetise as entrepreneurs of the self, why can we not get rid of it? What would it mean to truly be free to construct a self? This is the utopian horizon of the horror story that is the biography of JT Leroy.

19

more or less matter

Kevin Breathnach

the effect that crowds
mon pauvre être nerveux

Not long after their arrival in Rome at the start of April 1867, the brothers Edmond and Jules de Goncourt noted, in a journal entry anticipating the style if not the sensibility of Thomas Bernhard, that *everything that is beautiful here is beautiful in a course, material way.* The pair would stay for six weeks, touring the city's galleries with an eye that seemed in no way softened by the languors of travel: Raphael's *Transfiguration* is reported to give the impression of wallpaper, while his *Resurrection* is judged *purely academic. This, a supernatural event, a divine legend? I know no canvas which depicts it in a commoner prose, a more vulgar beauty.* And it's true: for a recently resurrected body, Raphael's Christ does seem kind of jaded, but I'm less interested in the value or the vehemence of the brothers' judgement here, than in the way the *Journal* slides, as it often does elsewhere, so casually and without warning, from the first-person *plural* to the first-person *singular*. After their mother's death in 1848, the brothers were apart for more than twenty-four hours only twice. While working together on their novels, plays, art criticism and journal entries, Jules would hold the pen while Edmond — eight years the elder — stood behind him, pacing back and forth, leaning over his shoulder with suggestions. *It is impossible to attribute any entry to one or the other,* their translator notes. Theirs is an *I* containing more than itself. It is a singular pronoun of multitudes. It is a crowd, a site of excess.

✡

When the Goncourts visited the Vatican during Holy Week that summer, they were struck by the *sly ecclesiastical malice* they believed the prelates put into *humiliating and torturing the foreigner's curiosity.* Sceptics of high-standing and sickly dispositions — each one tortured all their life by the other's stomach, liver and nerve complaints — the brothers did not appreciate having to queue outside in the blistering heat of their Roman holiday, sometimes for hours at a time. Once inside the Museo Pio Clementino, however, the two were left awe-struck before a two-thousand-year-old fragment of a nude male statue which they refer to as the Vatican *Torso.* Believed to represent Ajax contemplating suicide, the fragment is signed with a name that's mentioned nowhere else in any surviving ancient literature or art: this is all that remains of Apollonius, son of Nestor, his entire output lost except for this, a piece of work that's largely lost as well. The figure has no head or neck or arms, no feet or calves or shins. It has nothing but a squat marble cock-and-balls; two muscular marble thighs; and of course that abdomen, that perfect marble abdomen, created with such sympathy, such skill, that the Goncourts — writing not only in the *Journal,* but in their book of criticism, *L'Art du 18ème siècle* — would hail the *Torso* as *the only fragment of art in the world which has given us the complete and absolute feeling of being a work of art.* What got the brothers going here was not the myth of the thing, nor the lyricism of an allegory half-told, but rather, the way in which the surface of the represented abdomen — that twisted torso, its muscles tensed — had given them both to imagine the processes taking place beneath it: *this fragment of breathing chest,* they write, *these palpitating entrails in this digesting stomach.* For all that's lacking here, for all the ravages of oblivion that this body has incurred, what we have is a work of art, a piece of matter, that gives no sense of less, but of *more*.

✵

The Goncourts returned to Paris just long enough for Théophile Gautier to introduce them to an upscale Champs-Élysées brothel *(its extravagant Renaissance decoration in the worst possible taste)* before they headed south again, this time to Vichy, a place where they report *one loses the illusion that sickness is a distinction.* Nine days into the trip, the brothers read that the poet François Ponsard has died. Sickness was the spirit of the age, as the *Journal* will reflect when they return to Paris, becoming more and more a catalogue of visits paid by friends to the city's many doctors and specialists. Not until the last months of 1869, however, do the horrifying symptoms of tertiary syphilis — a disease contracted by Jules, an enthusiastic patron of brothels, as many as fifteen years before — show up in the text and take hold of it.

✵

18 October, 1869. *Left Trouville after spending twenty days there, the worst twenty days of our lives.*

✵

1 November. *The agony of being ill and unable to be ill at home, of having to drag one's pain and weakness from one place to another.*

✵

14 December. *Nervous illness transforms all moral pain into physical pain, such that the body suffers a second time what the soul has already suffered.*

✡

The entries in 1870 are shorter, fewer. 1 January. *Today, the first day of the year, no calls, none of our friends, nobody: solitude and suffering.*

✡

10 January, another short entry. *Dizziness, uneasiness, a sort of terror: such is the effect that crowds have today on my poor nervous system.*

✡

A little later in the century, syphilis would manage to acquire what Susan Sontag described as *darkly positive associations*—a whole artistic mythos concerning feverish mental states and creative spells—but such glamour had yet to attach itself to the disease when Jules first noticed the early tell-tale chancre. His affliction is never named as anything more specific than a *nervous illness,* but the brothers would have had a pretty clear sense, not only of what the disease was, but of the hell it was about to visit upon Jules. After two years in a semi-paralytic state, unable to understand or formulate language, Charles Baudelaire had died, ruined by syphilis, in a *maison de santé* in 1867.

✡

Only one more entry is made after 10 January before the pen falls from Jules's hand: a long final showing in which it is reported that, in the late-stages of his own nervous illness, the composer Vaucorbeil had developed a horror of all things velvet. *My poor nervous system* would be the last phrase Jules wrote with the first-person singular outside quotation marks: *our* lives, *one's* pain, *our* friends, but *my* poor nervous system. The switch to the first-person singular seems far less casual here than usual. For here their *I* splits open, becomes discrete. Here sickness is a distinction. For once it's clearly Jules who speaks, who speaks *in* and *of* and *for* himself; who *screams* in fact, desperate to make one last mark that's all his own, a single phrase will do, a fragment to survive him, a figure with no neck or head, no arms or feet or shins, no excess and yet *more: mon pauvre être nerveux.*

✵

For the next six months, Jules will read aloud from Chateaubriand's *Memoires d'outre tombe* more and more obsessively, oblivious to his brother's indifference to it, but still oppressively conscious of his own decline. By June he has forgotten the name of every book they'd written together, yet he remains lucid enough to feel shame. On Saturday, 11 June, Jules manoeuvres a bowl clumsily in a restaurant. *It's not my fault,* he cries across the table, where in tears he continues with cryptic incoherence: *I know how it upsets you, but I often want to and I can't.* The following weekend, on 18 June, Jules will suffer a stroke that leaves him bedridden for two days: his body thrashing round in horrifying pain, sleepless and mute; his mind haunted by some apparition in the curtain which he does not have the words to describe. *A disintegration of the brain had occurred at the base of the skull,* says the doctor. Not until the second stroke hits him will he die.

✵

The night of Sunday–Monday, 19–20 June. *All night long, that rasping sound of breathing like the sound of a saw cutting through wet wood, punctuated every now and then by heart-rending groans and plaintive cries. All night long, that beating and heaving of his chest against the sheet.*

✵

Monday, nine at night. *I touch his hands: they are like moist marble.*

✡

Monday, twenty to ten. *He is dying, he has died. God be praised, he died after two or three gentle breaths, like a child falling asleep. How frightful is the immobility of this body under the sheets, no longer rising and falling with the gentle movement of respiration, no longer living the life of sleep.*

✡

That rasping chest. Those hands *like marble. The immobility of his body under the sheets.* These states and textures always make me think of the Torso which the brothers so admired. *A sublime work of art,* they called it, *which derives its beauty from the living representation of life.* Though the account of Jules's death-agony is very bleak and often gruesome, it is unquestionably beautiful as well, a sublime work of art which, since its existence was a secret to everyone until 1883, it is difficult, maybe impossible, to date exactly. In the italicised passage just after Jules's final entry, Edmond is no more specific than to tell us that it had been *an interval of many months* before he took up *the pen fallen from my brother's fingers.* For at least nine months in any case, the immediacy that so marked the writing of the first nineteen years is lost, sacrificed in the service of *recounting to myself the story of his death-agony and despair.* These sheets in which Jules dies are backdated: the work of memory, moments recollected with the help of notes jotted down during nights of distress and so *comparable to those cries by which we relieve the pain of great physical suffering.* Inscribed into these lines is the echo of that suffering, those cries. For the I inhabiting them is a voice in which lurks an absence, something that was there but is not; a voice grown echoic in its emptiness. These sheets derive their beauty from *the deathly representation of dying.* Here is an account of a death, told by a voice that holds this death inside it.

20

Sylvia Plath

Emily LaBarge

I AM NO SHADOW[1]

Face in obscurity, she blows out three white candles that burn at different lengths, fixed to a saucer sitting atop a desk crowded with papers. Streams of smoke rise into the air; thin white lines twist and coil, undulating against the darkness of the surrounding room.

From behind, we see her walk up a short flight of stairs into the kitchen. Backlit with early morning glow, she emerges in silhouette — tall, slender, modest housecoat tied at the waist, long hair hanging down her back — as she moves in a deliberate, efficient manner. She opens and closes cupboards, prepares a tray of tea for one, pauses to look out the large window from where she can see the milkman begin his daily rounds.

Back at the desk, her hands pull a sheet of paper out of a typewriter — neat two line stanzas run down the length of white — gently fingering its edges before turning to pick up a cup of coffee and switch off the radio.

---

1 Sylvia Plath, 'Three Women: A Poem for Three Voices', in *Collected Poems*, ed. Ted Hughes (New York: Harper and Row, 1981), 187.

In the kitchen again, her hands and fingers again, up close as they peel carrots and potatoes, boil pots of water — roiling liquid, rising steam.

Again on the stairs, again walking up in the dim light, and past, and away, always away, and in shadow, from us, where we wait, below. Features invisible, she passes quickly, a baby held against her hip, and ascends to a bathroom where she kneels down on the bare tiles and leans forward to place the infant in the tub.

Outside, grey day, from afar, again the elegant silhouette. Too distant to make out anything clearly. She pushes a pram up a steep green incline, a small child in red scampers behind. Later, she stands alone on the bald hill, the bare black arms of trees snake around her, framing the flat sky.

The black horse whinnies and bucks. From the shoulders down the woman cuts a dark profile against the sun that glints in the distance as she rides, in slow-motion. She pulls in the reigns, feet firmly in stirrups, as her body rises and falls with each gallop. A glimpse of fine jawline, cheekbone, nose, long strands of hair whipping in the wind, before she is eclipsed by the surging light and surrounding scape.

A woman is dragging her shadow in a circle
About a bald hospital saucer.
It resembles the moon, or a sheet of blank paper
And appears to have suffered a sort of private blitzkrieg.[2]

Who is this woman? This shadowy figure, dark remainder, spectral penumbra? The credits tell me she is Sally Sinclair, with her two children, starring as Sylvia Plath and *her* two children, in *Voices & Visions*, a 13-part television series about poets, produced in the late 1980s by the New York Center for Visual History. The programme runs just under an hour and consists primarily of

2 Plath, 'A Life', in *Collected Poems*, 49.

interviews with family, acquaintances, literary critics and fellow poets. These clips sit alongside a collage of static archival images — from photographs to letters, journal entries and working drafts of poems — interspersed with dramatic vignettes in which the speculative outline of Plath goes about her daily routine, face in shadow or head cut off entirely, omitted by the viewfinders' exacting frame. Headless, her dark body makes its way heedless: animated by voiceovers and anecdotes, she rises and rises again, and again, *at about four in the morning — that still blue, almost eternal hour before the baby's cry, before the glassy music of the milkman, settling his bottles.*[3]

The documentary opens with a statement about Plath, who 'lived in London and died last Monday'. The voice and the voiceover are unidentified, and it took me some time to realise that this is a snippet from one of only a few obituaries for Plath — written for *The Observer* by her friend, the poet and critic A. Alvarez, and broadcast on BBC Third Programme shortly after her death — with the result that the first time I watched it, I was astonished that the piece could have been made so quickly. From where did they get the manuscripts? And all the archival sources? How did they rapidly generate the ideas for, not to mention film the bizarre biographical interpretation scenes — the beekeepers and the candles, girls in togas with wreathes of flowers, grey ponies on even greyer moors? Moreover, how were all of these people sitting there, just days following her death, discussing her life and work so calmly, betraying little to no emotion, presenting confident, case-closed analyses of her intentions both literary and personal?

And yet, while the film was in fact made nearly 30 years after Plath's death in 1963, aged 30, it betrays hallmarks — both tonally and structurally — of most of the critical documents about

3 Sylvia Plath, quoted by A. Alvarez in *The Art of Sylvia Plath,* ed. Charles Newman (Bloomington: Indiana University Press, 1970), 59.

the poet produced from the years following the publication of her posthumous collection *Ariel,* in 1965, up until present day.

Experts brought forward as witnesses.

Close friends and family who speak of the highs the lows the strangeness the difficult nature— *When she was eight years old she saw the new moon and murmured to herself, 'the moon is a lock of witch's hair—and the night winds pause and stare at that strand from a witch's head.*[4] The death drive, the melancholy, the crashing crushing force of energy— *She loved to show her scars and tell her stories of smashing on the basement floor, whatever it was, and the life force, the life force in her was so strong it counteracted all those pills she'd taken.*[5]

Detractors who, smiling and self-assured, detail the volatility, the lack of a certain *gentility* (British shorthand for American): she was a genius but but but she destroyed herself and everything around her and she oh she *needed* it, she *wanted* it—everything for the poetry, the wicked poetry with its blood and its bones, anguished visions and violent shrieks.

Critics who stand in awe of the prolific nature of her final output, fast and furious: a book of poems in roughly a year, many of the finest within under two months. Fellow writers who wince to think of the drive and the discipline, as well as the fierce loneliness and the wilful, resigned isolation.

Other critics who chide and sneer: couldn't have been *that* bad, Sylvia! What a morbid woman, what a singularly not nice girl. No wonder she—

---

4 Aurelia Plath, quoted in *Voice & Visions: Sylvia Plath* (New York: New York Center for Visual History, 1988), https://www.learner.org/catalog/extras/vvspot/Plath.html.

5 Clarissa Roche, quoted in *Voices & Visions.*

Hackneyed visions of what it might have been like on *that horse,* in *that flat,* in *her mind,* and *those final days.* The body trotted out, sometimes even with her pony, to answer for itself over and over.

Plath's poems are often read as a key to her death, a pre-post-humous text actively scripted to close with the grand finale of suicide — urgently resonant in its harbinger of an event that had already passed by the time the collection could be read as a whole. To me, they have always spoken as uncanny premonitions of the events that would follow: all manner of conjuring, mythology, exorcism, visitation to be exacted upon her body, her — corpus — of — work — intellect — interior — mind — heart — life —

In *The Bell Jar,* Plath's protagonist Esther lies in bed unable to sleep and muses, *I thought the most beautiful thing in the world must be shadow, the million moving shapes and cul-de-sacs of shadow. There was shadow in bureau drawers and closets and suitcases, and shadow under houses and trees and stones, and shadow at the back of people's eyes and smiles, and shadow, miles and miles and miles of it, on the night side of the earth.*[6] In a world, a body and a mind that feels hot, cramped, empty and sizzling with fearful torpor, shadow is a welcome relief: the cool dark beneath the hard slick, the heart of darkness that lurks within, blurred contours, unknowing, distance, mystery preserved. Sally Sinclair, with her silly silhouette and her shaded face, her headless mannequin, is one of many instances in which Plath-after-death is resurrected only to be actively denied many of these things, frozen in both shadow and light. As the poet herself wrote, *Nobody watched me before, now I am watched... Once a day the light slowly widens and slowly thins, / And I see myself, flat, ridiculous, a cut-paper shadow.*[7]

6 Sylvia Plath, *The Bell Jar* (London: Faber and Faber, 1978), 155.

7 Plath, 'Tulips', in *Collected Poems*, 160.

THERE ARE TWO OF ME NOW[8]

That is to say: divided. More than two, I would say—but of course a set of mirror reflections can ricochet into infinity. A popular Plath-itude is the idea of the 'divided self', put forward by her husband Ted Hughes (and other critics following his suit): for most of her existence, she was dogged by the coincidence of two warring selves—the artificial and the authentic—who violently clashed in both her work and her life. Poetry, like life in general, is full of shackles and expectations, rules, strictures that obscure the real self, the real expression at the centre, wherein lies the difficult truth of the matter—of *all* matters: *THE THINGS OF THE WORLD WITH NO GLAZING.*[9] Is this a perilous wager, particularly where poetry is concerned?

Linda Wagner Martin writes: *For a young woman to kill herself at the beginning of a successful writing career posed an intriguing and frightening mystery. All kinds of equations between art and life began to be suggested. Had Plath written so personally that she had somehow crossed the boundary between art and life? Was full exploration of the creative process dangerous?*[10] Never mind the troubling myth of wholeness, which disallows for a self in fragments and encourages the notion of a drive towards (and the possibility of) an ultimate synthesis; but what is the boundary between art and life? To what ends does this binary serve? And by what rite, right, write of passage might one attain—*who by fire, who by water*[11]—the glistening at the centre, *the pure gold baby.*[12]

---

8 Plath, 'In Plaster', in *Collected Poems*, 158.

9 Sylvia Plath, *The Unabridged Journals of Sylvia Plath*, ed. Karen V. Kukil (New York: Anchor Books, 2000), 485.

10 Linda Wagner Martin, ed., *Sylvia Plath: The Critical Heritage* (London: Routledge, 1988), 1.

11 Leonard Cohen, 'Who by Fire', *New Skin for the Old Ceremony* (Sound Ideas Studio, CBS-69087, 1974)

12 Plath, 'Lady Lazarus', in *Collected Poems*, 244.

Is there something bare and burned about poetry — *playing with fire* — that it can sear its stark, minimal truths into your flesh until you are flayed, the skin hangs off in strips and you — *who by high ordeal, who by common trial*[13] — kneel down and you bow under the creaking weight and you worry that if the tension keeps up, the heat and the pressure, you will tear in half, wilt in two with a terrible red sigh.

Sliced in two like a flatfish, each of us is perpetually hunting for the matching half of himself.[14]

Split, slit right down the middle — incised.

Cut — slash — burn. The ruthless mantra of many a great writer. And the gore at the core is nothing but — your heart — your authentic self — a truly selfless offering — that comes at a price nonetheless. Scatter the remains to the wind.

WHO HAS DISMEMBERED US?[15]

Printed on 17 February 1963, Alvarez's obituary for Plath was entitled 'A Poet's Epitaph'. As would many after, Alvarez wrote as though the poet had lost an arduous battle with language: *For the last few months she had been writing continuously, almost as though possessed. In these last poems, she was systematically probing that narrow, violent area between the viable and the impossible, between experience which can be transmuted into poetry and that which is overwhelming.*[16]

Alongside his text were printed four poems — 'Edge', 'The Fearful', 'Kindness' and 'Contusion' — and a picture of Plath holding her baby son, Nicholas. Over the poet's shoulder,

13 Cohen, 'Who by Fire'.
14 Aristophanes, quoted in Anne Carson, *Eros the Bittersweet* (Princeton: Princeton University Press, 1988), 31.
15 Plath, 'Event', in *Collected Poems*, 195.
16 A. Alvarez, 'A Poet's Epitaph', *Weekend Observer*, 17 February 1963, 23.

behind her dark hair and her hesitant smile, is a poster of Isis — goddess of nature and magic, friend to artisans, sinners and slaves — which is said to have presided over Plath's writing desk. The Egyptian myth of Isis describes her collecting and reassembling the scattered parts of her lover, Osiris, after he is murdered and dismembered by his evil brother, Set. It is this theme that underlines the astrological meaning of Isis as the bringing together of fragments, resurrection and re-membering. Isis endures — her name repeats the present tense of the verb 'to be': Is, Is. A sentiment echoed in *The Bell Jar*'s Esther, who — attending the funeral of an old peer — hears the 'old brag' of her heart: *I am, I am, I am.*[17]

In the poem 'Event', Plath's narrator laments the opening of a 'black gap' that love can no longer enter. *My limbs, also, have left me,* she notes, before asking with blank surprise, *Who has dismembered us?*[18] She seems to understand the perilous knife-edge of curiosity, the injustice it can carve into living things, reaching for intimacies that unmask not knowledge but rather *the isolate, slow faults / That kill, that kill, that kill.*[19]

At her death, Plath left a completed manuscript, entitled *Ariel,* which she had carefully arranged to begin with the word 'Love', in a poem about the birth of her daughter, and to end with the word 'Spring', in the final of the 'bee poems', 'Wintering', which speaks of endurance, hibernation and rebirth. Her intestate death resulted in the rights of all her work and materials being passed to her husband at the time, Ted Hughes, who reordered and edited the manuscript to form the famous collection we now know by the same name.

Hughes' *Ariel* omitted 13 of Plath's choices and included 13 of his in their stead — many of them from a handful of poems she

17 Plath, *The Bell Jar,* 256.

18 Plath, 'Event', in *Collected Poems,* 195.

19 Plath, 'Elm', in *Collected Poems,* 193.

had written in the days leading immediately to her death. In his introduction to the *Collected Poems,* he qualifies his actions as practical editorial decisions: he is the keeper of Plath's work, and responsible for its creative integrity, distribution and reception. *Several advisers,* he tells us, *had felt that the violent contradictory feelings expressed in those pieces might prove hard for the reading public to take. In one sense, as it turned out, this apprehension showed some insight.*[20] He explains further that he also *omitted some of the more personally aggressive poems from 1962, and might have omitted one or two more if she had not already published them herself in magazines — so that by 1965 they were widely known.*[21]

Amongst these 'personally aggressive' poems that *were* included are 'Daddy' and 'Lady Lazarus', both of which Plath had read for a BBC broadcast in October 1962, as well as sought publication for around the same time, and which are now considered to be some of the best poems of the 20th century. To a degree, the 'apprehension' seems misguided: the contradictory impulses — the violence, the jarring tension and uncanny, uncomfortable images — are what Plath has become known for and was, arguably, working incredibly hard to achieve, with little regard for whether the reading public would easily 'take' them or not.

So what exactly is the concern? Who is afraid of Sylvia Plath?

Others of the omitted poems would be published in later volumes, *Crossing the Water* and *Winter Trees,* but some — particularly those that make veiled reference to difficult elements of the Plath–Hughes relationship (they separated in the summer of 1962 and were arranging to divorce at the time of Plath's decease) — would not see the published page until *The Collected Poems,* 1981.

---

20 Ted Hughes, 'Introduction' to Plath, *Collected Poems,* 15.
21 Ibid.

Cut cut cut — cut it back — parse — chop — hide — cut it again — parcel — neatly in — brown — paper — tied with a — hope the — insides don't — seep —

Difficult. *Difficult. She was very difficult.*[22]

Until *Ariel* was published by Faber & Faber in 1965, the circumstances of Plath's death were not widely known: she was said to have 'died suddenly' — only friends, family and close peers would have known of her early morning suicide by gas oven, and even fewer the lonely particulars of two children in a sealed off nursery room upstairs, plates of bread and butter, glasses of milk carefully laid out in case they got hungry before someone else arrived.

The late poems that Hughes chose to include in his editorial re-arrangement, those written in the weeks leading up to her death, and which Plath felt to be the beginning of another body of work, are excellent. They are also stark, chilling, sinister, cold and resigned. As arranged in the collection, and in light of the surrounding circumstances, instead of Plath's original difficult but ultimately triumphant voice, *Ariel* reads like an expertly crafted suicide script in which the final page is really the final page, the end of the story, the last word, with Plath's corpse tumbling into guttered white silence after the ultimate full stop:

The woman is perfected
Her dead

Body wears the smile of accomplishment,
The illusion of a Greek necessity

Flows in the scrolls of her toga,
Her bare

22 A. Alvarez, quoted in *Voices & Visions: Sylvia Plath.*

Feet seem to be saying:
We have come so far, it is over.[23]

Here's what you asked for — your pretty package — gagged — no — I mean bound — stamped — a seal of — official —

Was it better that Plath seem a morbid and dangerous necromantic, hell-bent on self-destruction, than that she seem 'personally aggressive' or 'difficult'? Unkind, unpleasant, unfriendly, ungracious, unlikable — *ungrateful.* These are words that have governed the editing of Plath's entire body of work as though the thing to be preserved is a particular kind of woman, one that quite clearly resembles Plath no more in death than in life, rather than a particular kind of work or a creative voice, one that the poet herself intended to be heard.

But maybe she just didn't know any better.

She needed guidance. She needed someone else to tell her what she really wanted; what she really meant to say. To distinguish the real from the false.

This is the better book, oh dutiful apprentice, trust me, follow, and someday soon *I will discharge thee.*[24] This this this is what you sound like. This is what it looks like, the body you left behind.

Just lie — still — for a — it won't — hurt — or well — only — just — a bit —

Plath notoriously consulted Hughes on nearly everything she wrote, and often took 'writing assignments' from him, as he encouraged her to push herself and to continue to develop the

23 Plath, 'Edge', in *Collected Poems*, 272.

24 William Shakespeare, *The Tempest*, in *The Complete Works of William Shakespeare* (London: Scott, Webster, and Geary, 1842), I.II.231.

voice that he could hear buried beneath all of the neat structural preoccupations that governed much of her early work. Yet, in late journal entries, Plath writes things like, *Must try poems. DO NOT SHOW ANY TO TED. I sometimes feel a paralysis come over me: his opinion is so important to me. Didn't show him the bull one: a small victory.*[25] Hughes himself noted, following their separation, a sense of breaking free that Plath began to pursue more persistently in her work, perhaps pushing towards that 'authentic self' — one previous hindrance of which might have been the well-intentioned, but perhaps inadequate governing tutelage of her husband. Inadequate as in — limited. As in, what the poet Hughes might have thought Plath was, or could be, both in life and in death, might not have accorded with her own creative wishes and visions — her violent contradictions — her difficult, intemperate, unapologetic I.

We murder to dissect.[26]

These points and their many surrounding arguments, both populist and literary, are decades old and there is enough other literature to consult for the finer points. It is just to say, here, that it smarts to read private journals published with OMISSION — OMISSION — OMISSION — and endless strains of ellipses where the 'nasty', 'vicious', 'untrue' or, bizarrely, 'erotically limiting'[27] bits have been excised like malignant tumours in a manner that recalls Plath's 'The Surgeon at 2am',

It is a statue the orderlies are wheeling off.
I have perfected it.
I am left with an arm or a leg,
A set of teeth, or stones
To rattle in a bottle and take home,

25 Plath, *Unabridged Journals*, 467.

26 William Wordsworth, 'The Tables Turned', in *Lyrical Ballads: With a Few Other Poems* (London: Biggs and Cottle, 1798), 180.

27 Frances McCullough, 'Editor's Note', in Sylvia Plath, *The Journals of Sylvia Plath*, ed. Frances McCullough (New York: Random House, 1982), xii.

And tissue in slices—a pathological salami.
Tonight the parts are entombed in an icebox.
Tomorrow they will swim
In vinegar like saint's relics.
Tomorrow the patient will have a clean, pink plastic limb.[28]

I guess, at the end of the day, no one likes a big mess.

The evidence is ample, here and elsewhere in life, that we do not always know how to care for one we might love, or have loved. We do not always understand or want to see who they struggle to become, for this is unknown even to them. Those who can no longer speak must be protected and yes, to a degree, spoken for. But might we find a way even so to let the body remain as it is — intact — even as it yawns with cavernous fissures and rotten flesh? For this partial wholeness is less dangerous than one that places a cold cast death mask over the face and says, I saw, I see, I say, I speak, I knew, I know — the truth, what she wanted, or would have, had she really known herself — here — in this — charnel house —

Nights, I squat in the cornucopia,
Of your left ear, out of the window,

Counting the red stars and those of plum-color.
The sun rises under the pillar of your tongue.[29]

In 'The Colossus', Plath's narrator is the caretaker of an inert giant who quietly looms ominous and omnipresent, a dead weight. She describes the tender machinations required to labour over the landscape of his body, *Scaling little ladders with gluepots and pails of Lysol / I crawl like an ant in mourning / Over the weedy*

28 Plath, 'The Surgeon at 2 a.m.', in *Collected Poems*, 170.
29 Plath, 'The Colossus', in *Collected Poems*, 130.

acres of your brow / To mend the immense skull-plates and clear / The bald, white tumuli from your eyes.[30]

Bones, whiteness, bald and hard, faceless skulls play a central role in Plath's imagery. The moon is *white as a knuckle and terribly upset,*[31] she watches from the sky where she *has nothing to be sad about, / Staring from her hood of bone. // She is used to this sort of thing. Her blacks crackle and drag.*[32] There is everywhere the sense of a *bonewhite light, like death, behind all things*[33] that sears the bleached O-gape of bone sockets fulsome with emptiness that nonetheless harbours, with cool desolation, a person who murmurs sweet entreaties into the ear of a deaf giant. There is a whispering along the bones — a creature that scratches for the honey at the centre of the marrow comb, a voice *that does not know what it has done to deserve baldness, errors, infidelities,*[34] but wants to get to the bottom of *the deep tap roo*t to find out.

THERE IS A CHARGE[35]

'Johnny Panic and the Bible of Dreams' tells the story of a young girl who works as Assistant to the Secretary in an Out-Patient Department of a Clinic Building at the City Hospital, where her job is primarily to type up records. In these records she finds described the dreams of patients, in which she feels she can see at work, coursing, the major force of the world — panic: *Panic with a dog-face, devil-face, hag-face, whore-face, panic in capital letters with no face at all — it's the same Johnny Panic, awake or asleep.* Feeling she understands the rich blue veins, the deep truth currents of panic that run everywhere just under the skin, she anoints herself 'dream connoisseur', faithful servant to Johnny

30 Ibid., 129.

31 Plath, 'The Moon and the Yew Tree', in *Collected Poems,* 173.

32 Plath, 'Edge', in *Collected Poems,* 272.

33 Plath, 'Insomniac', in *Collected Poems,* 163.

34 Donald Barthelme, 'The Indian Uprising', in *Sixty Stories* (London: Penguin, 2003), 104.

35 Plath, 'Lady Lazarus', in *Collected Poems,* 246.

Panic, for whom she will compile the Bible of Dreams — the motto of which reads: *Perfect fear casteth out all else.*[36]

By day she is just a regular working girl: no one can see the dark, frayed knowledge that scores through her centre. By night, she hatches a plan to stay in the hospital record room overnight, a marathon run at her dutiful transcriptions. When she is found out, the Clinic Director and his baleful assistant take her to a cold white room where she is undressed, robed in white sheets, extended on a cot and held down: *the crown of wire is placed on my head, the wafer of forgetfulness on my tongue.*[37] As the machine begins to whir and the orderlies stand over her reciting a devotional chant about fear, the girl sees the face of Johnny Panic and she is *shaken like a leaf in the teeth of glory…His Word charges and illumines the universe. The air crackles with his blue-tongued lightning-haloed angels…He Forgets not his own.*[38] Even as the girl is punished for her dark truths and insights, she prevails — by them, through them, in them she is exalted — still waters run deep.

There is a question to be posed, in writing as elsewhere, about who benefits from certain varieties of silences and forgetfulness. About what kind of anaesthetic is really necessary — and who should be given the power — and the choice — to administer it. To determine who and when and how needs to be softened around the edges and why, which is not always for her — his, their, your, our — own good.

I love the locust tree
the sweet white locust
            How much?

36 Sylvia Plath, 'Johnny Panic and the Bible of Dreams', in *Johnny Panic and the Bible of Dreams* (Cutchogue: Buccaneer Books, 1994), 160.

37 Ibid., 166.

38 Ibid.

How much?
How much does it cost
to love the locust tree
in bloom?[39]

The notion of cost is an interesting one. It's true that we do pay for things, in all manner of ways, sometimes dearly. William Carlos Williams' poem seems to address the cost of beauty, perhaps where poetry is concerned: how much will be lost or gained in attempting to love the locust tree in bloom, in person, in mind, in words.

In a *New York Review of Books* essay, 'On Sylvia Plath', Elizabeth Hardwick writes, *But even in recollection — and* The Bell Jar *was written more than a decade after the happenings — Sylvia Plath does not ask the cost.*[40] In this case, I am unclear as to what is being addressed: the cost of what? Hardwick describes the voice of Plath's fiction and poetry as destructive, paranoid, angry, bitter, vengeful, arrogant, suffering, ungenerous and aggressive — qualities that she describes as 'reckless'; but again: reckless with what? What is the gamble? What is at stake? Hardwick seems to suggest not only that the use of difficult or challenging autobiographical material for inspiration exacts a price from the writer, but that particular *kinds* of writing — language, tone, imagery — are dangerous, and possibly even morally or ethically erroneous, for writer and reader alike.

In an interview with Peter Orr, Plath described poetry as a 'tyrannical discipline', *you've got to go so far, so fast, in such a small space you just have to burn away all the peripherals.*[41] Who is it, then? Who pays for the idea that if poetry goes too far, too

39 William Carlos Williams, 'The Library', in *Paterson* (New York: New Directions, 1992), 95.

40 Elizabeth Hardwick, 'On Sylvia Plath', *The New York Review of Books*, 12 August, 1971, http://www.nybooks.com/articles/1971/08/12/on-sylvia- plath/.

41 Sylvia Plath, 'A 1962 Interview with Peter Orr', in *The Poet Speaks: Interviews with Contemporary Poets Conducted by Hilary Morrish, Peter Orr,*

fast, in too small a space, it carries the price tag of a human life? Who benefits from the closing of the gap between things that inspire work and the final work itself, replacing the imaginative space with a body or a fractured psyche that cannot withstand productive osmosis?

Later in the same interview, Plath explains, *I think my poems immediately come out of the sensuous and emotional experiences I have, but I must say I cannot sympathise with these cries from the heart that are informed by nothing except a needle or a knife, or whatever it is. I believe that one should be able to control and manipulate experiences, even the most terrific, like madness, being tortured, this sort of experience...with an informed and intelligent mind. I think that personal experience is very important, but certainly it shouldn't be a kind of shut-box and mirror looking, narcissistic experience. I believe it should be* relevant, *and relevant to the larger things, the bigger things such as Hiroshima and Dachau and so on.*[42]

One of the more assiduous dissections of Plath's posthumous body has been the correlation of every known event in her life — either as noted in her journals, or remembered by (a select number of) the people who knew her — with her creative work. A leads directly to B with little to no room for interpretation or imagination on the part of poet and reader alike and 'misreadings' are corrected with citations of the 'truth', as in the notes that accompany 'Death & Co.' in *The Collected Poems.* Plath's introduction for a BBC reading is cited, and explains, *This poem is about the double or schizophrenic nature of death — the marmoreal coldness of Blake's death mask, say, hand in glove with the fearful softness of worms, water and other katabolists. I imagine these two aspects of death as two men, two business friends who have come to call.* Underneath her statement is a correction from

John Press, and Ian Scott-Kilvery. (London: Routledge, 1966), http://www.english.illinois.edu/maps/poets/m_r/plath/orrinterview.htm.

42 Ibid.

the collection's omniscient narrator: *The actual occasion was a visit by well-meaning men who invited* TH *[Ted Hughes] to live abroad at a tempting salary, and whom she therefore resented.*[43]

Must we read such a poem as having an 'actual occasion'? Is it redundant to declare the truth content of a creative document? In what circumstances must a writer and her narrator(s) or voices, her life and her work be considered one and the same? In this rendering of Plath's body of work, where is the current, the blue jolt volt — the *charge* at the core — the insistent beating of the heart, you can hear it, *It really goes*[44] — the crackle, sizzle, burn of something rising out of itself? Where is the poet with her great discipline and mastery of difficult experience, her refusal of narcissism, her ability to imagine beyond literal transcriptions of the every day, to transcend, to create: *to write.*

In Plath's work, the charge that electrocutes — burns bare along the nerve — is also the charge that electrifies the imagination, tears open the plain surfaces to reveal the surging, essential, often difficult truths of being human as a state that inevitably involves moments of pain and suffering. The daily acknowledgement of these aspects of life has been chosen by many as a critical, imperative pursuit within creative work — one for which there is no price or threat of personal annihilation, but rather the reward of evolution and endurance.

It is this pact that Plath forges with her readers when she invites them for *The big strip tease./ Gentleman, ladies,* and when she charges them, *a very large charge / For a word or a touch / Or a bit of blood.*[45] The voice of Ariel as a whole is notable for its hard disdain and lack of self-pity, its blank, nursery rhyme taunts. It is this voice, which asks for nothing, that *the peanut-crunching*

43 Plath, 'Notes: 1962', in *Collected Poems,* 294.
44 Plath, 'Lady Lazarus', in *Collected Poems,* 246.
45 Ibid., 245–46.

crowd[46] hears and follows nonetheless because it dares to make unsavoury promises: come with me and I'll show you. And they do and they have and they probably always will. Not even Wordsworth thought poetry was all clouds and daffodils.

Without this charge, it is no wonder that when she rises from the table Plath lurches, unsteady and bewildered, recalling the empty, imprisoned figures of her own work: 'The Applicant' who is presented with *A living doll, everywhere you look. / It can sew, it can cook, / It can talk, talk, talk.*[47] — or 'The Munich Mannequins' who, in their barren perfection, in their sulphur loveliness, in their smiles, lean *Naked and bald in their furs, / Orange lollies on silver sticks, // Intolerable, without mind.*[48]

The sutures stretch and tear where the thread is pulled too tightly, stiches uneven and hasty, recalling Mary Shelley's description of *Frankenstein* as her 'hideous progeny'.[49] Shelley's monster is monstrous not because of his literal monstrousness, but because he reveals to us our impoverished and unenlightened nature upon beholding difference that we find terrifying because of its proximity to our own. Running on either side of this fine line, both human and monster suffer and grow in strength, in equal measure: for they are intimately bound. And the body exhumed can never again be made whole.

THE SPINE BONES BARED FOR A MOMENT[50]

There is this cave
In the air behind my body
That nobody is going to touch:
A cloister, a silence

---

46 Ibid.

47 Plath, 'The Applicant', in *Collected Poems*, 222.

48 Plath, 'The Munich Mannequins', in *Collected Poems*, 263.

49 Mary Shelley, 'Appendix I: Introduction to Shelley's 1831 Edition', in *Frankenstein* (Peterborough: Broadview Editions, 2012), 351.

50 Plath, 'Zoo-Keeper's Wife', in *Collected Poems*, 154.

Closing around a blossom of fire.
When I stand upright in the wind,
My bones turn to dark emeralds.[51]

It has taken me almost two years to understand how to write this essay. Never more have I wished I had read only primary and no secondary sources—the words of Plath alone, which had always meant so much to me, and nothing else surrounding. A litany of bony voices rises out of the warring remains like the endless question mark of a spine—with all of its fluids and delicate systems of nerves exposed, slender tangents of ribs winging faint chimes. So many tender possibilities for paralysis, trapped between knobby truths and impossible contradictions.

Never more have I found it more difficult to finish something as the words keep running keep keep running down and down and make more and less and un- and deeply- and never- and none- and all-important sense. Running down the middle of the middle, the heart of the heart of the body, which is the spine, there is a stately column of vertebrae. A litanous backbone of adjectives that interlock and fuse together, keeping both the woman and the poems standing up straight, even as they sway and sometimes falter under the force of gravity. And the eyes — they can still move — but she does not — she cannot — she never — ever — speaks just — listens — and stares — and — stares — as they —

Luminous
Successful
Vulnerable
Brilliant
Unrelenting
Ungenerous
Bitter
Resentful

51 James Wright, 'The Jewel', in *The Branch Will Not Break* (Middletown: Wesleyan University Press, 1963), 17.

Self-destructive
Disturbing
Disturbed
Unkind
Ungrateful
Vicious
Appendectomy
Nasty
Wicked
Malicious
Problematic
Vehement
Passionate
Goal-oriented
Confident
Competitive
Lively
Excessive
Hungry
Greedy
Harrowing
Hysterical
Sinusitis
Aggressive
Vengeful
Wrathful
Remorseless
Cruel
Humiliating
Miscarriage
Manipulative
Capable
Tough
Punishing
Polite
Pretty
Attractive

Glamorous
Neat
Tidy
Clean
Young
Mother
Forceful
Brisk
Housewife
Plain
Mousy
Normal
Fever
Alert
Bright
Friendly
Insomnia
Distant
Composed
Anxiety
Blonde
Witty
American
Fresh
Charming
Depression
Controlled
Shameless
Shameful
Brave
Brazen
Powerful
Talented
Dangerous
Witch
Necromantic
Disciplined

Gaunt
Priestess
Possessed
Animal
Driven
Sick
Hateful
Vengeful
Reckless
Genius

In the last months of working on this essay, there was a rat living in my house. Every night, as I lay in bed reading, a persistent scratching, gnawing noise would emerge from the cabinet beneath the sink. Later, after I had shoved old jars and tin foil into the space from which I felt sure the rat came, my DIY solutions managed only to amplify the noise and there would be the sound—rather predictably—of clinking glass and scrunching metal. Traps and poison were placed around the house, and the scratching slowly grew more and more faint; but you could still hear the creature dragging itself through the walls. One night I heard it under the stairs, scrabbling violently, before a long silence; and in the morning, one last, long scratch ended in a tumbling sound that seemed to fall into the place beneath my sink, where the tell-tale jars were interned. Sitting at my desk all day, staring at these words on these pages, I thought I could smell a rat. And I also started to think the rat was me: there must be a reason, here and now, that it had chosen my home for its final resting place. The cupboard made a snickering noise each time I opened it to check for any signs of evidence, and I imagined the rat's invisible mouth curled back in a sick smile—grinning wider and wider with knowledge of my dark paranoia—his skin shrivelling and shrinking to expose row after row of teeth filed to points.

He's laughing at me, I thought. *He knows,* I knew.

This is just to say, critically, that I know I am in line with all of the other birds of Plath prey waiting to behold whatever it is that remains, even though I'm sure that by this point all of the best cuts have been sold. But I wait, I am still waiting, in any case. Like all of the others, I suppose I too say I do it for her, while I try to ignore the feeling that there is a scalpel trembling in my hand. And I try not to hear her on the BBC programme about American poets in England, 'What made you stay?', describing her attachment to British butcher shops:

And I have since become devoted to the British butcher shops and I'm — I'm not by any means an expert, but I think you have to know your cuts of meat and it's a rather creative process to choose them out of the animal almost on the hook and I think this is an experience that I — I really was deprived of in America.[52]

THE BLOOD JET IS POETRY[53]

Words, words, to stop the deluge through the thumbhole in the dike, Plath writes in her journal, 1958; and in a later entry, 1959, *what inner decisions, what inner murder or prison break must I commit if I want to speak from my true deep voice in writing? Where are my small incidents; the blood poured from the shoes?*[54] Writing is the pumping piston, the aorta, the deepest blue red viscous that animates, snakes and pulses and without which she — we — you — I — cannot live.

Words, blood, fluid, holes, fissures, open, pouring, gushing, breaking, striking, wounding, spurting, rising, running, spilling, *What a thrill —*[55] and language falls like *Axes / After whose*

52 Sylvia Plath, 'What Made You stay?', *A World of Sound,* BBC Home Service, 7 September 1962, 3.30pm.

53 Plath, 'Kindness', in *Collected Poems,* 270.

54 Plath, *Unabridged Journals,* 318, 368–69.

55 Sylvia Plath, 'Cut', in *Ariel* (London: Faber and Faber, 1965), 23.

stroke the wood rings, / And the echoes! / Echoes travelling / Off from the centre like horses.[56]

The echoes resound and return, *Words dry and riderless, / The indefatigable hoof-taps,*[57] evoking Plath's early morning horse rides in Devon. Her steed named Ariel appears in the eponymous poem as *God's lioness, / How one we grow,* on whom she is hauled through the air, incandescent in scarlet motion: *And I / Am the arrow, // The dew that flies / Suicidal, at one with the drive / Into the red // Eye, the cauldron of morning.*[58] The echoes and the words, the blade against wood and the feeling of a great force finally breaking loose, with a relished howl of freedom, also recall Ariel of *The Tempest,* who was for 12 years imprisoned in a cloven pine by the evil witch Sycorax. The spirit is freed by the magician Prospero, to whom he is then indentured to perform various deeds in order to gain his liberty. Only Plath's Ariel, 'Ariel', Ariel is wayward and knows her power — she pulses and strains in her confines, heaves and throbs and escapes, rather than slavishly awaiting the impoverished freedom bestowed by another. *And but one word with one of us?* she seems to taunt, knowing the risk at hand, *couple it with something; make it a word and a blow.*[59]

The blood jet is poetry,
There is no stopping it.[60]

In these late poems the voice rises to a fever pitch, surging alongside veins of bloodshot ore that pulse in rhythm and rhyme. Alvarez remembers Plath's insistence upon sharing new work with him, late in 1962, that the poems be read out loud: *I want*

---

56 Plath, 'Words', in *Ariel,* 86.
57 Ibid.
58 Plath, 'Ariel', in *Ariel,* 37.
59 Shakespeare, *Romeo and Juliet,* in *The Complete Works of William Shakespeare,* III.I.39–40.
60 Plath, 'Kindness', in *Ariel,* 83.

you to hear *them.*[61] Hardwick, too, remembers attending a reading at which *these bitter poems were 'beautifully' read, projected in full-throated, plump, diction-perfect, Englishy, mesmerizing cadences, all round and rapid, and paced and spaced…Clearly, perfectly, staring you down.*[62] The dybbuk speaks: the voice rises and rises: a bloody ventriloquism that breaks the levy, streams through the dike: inside pours forth to outside: joyful excrescence, ecstatic filth.

In a letter to her mother, Plath wrote, *I shall be one of the few women poets in the world who is a fully rejoicing woman…I am a woman and glad of it, and my songs will be of the fertility of the earth.*[63] That her songs taste of *Black sweet blood mouthfuls,*[64] that their voices ring idiosyncratic, unconventional, uncanny and — to some — unacceptable, is a triumphant affirmation.

THE HEART HAS NOT STOPPED[65]

In the desert
I saw a creature, naked, bestial,
Who, squatting upon the ground,
Held his heart in his hands,
And ate of it.
I said, "Is it good, friend?"
"It is bitter—bitter," he answered;

"But I like it
"Because it is bitter,
"And because it is my heart."[66]

61 A. Alvarez, quoted in *Voice & Visions: Sylvia Plath.*
62 Hardwick, 'On Sylvia Plath'.
63 Sylvia Plath, *Letters Home* (New York: Harper & Row, 1975), 256.
64 Plath, 'Ariel', in *Ariel,* 36.
65 Plath, 'Mystic', in *Collected Poems,* 269.
66 Stephen Crane, 'In the Desert', in *The Complete Poems of Stephen Crane* (Ithaca: Cornell University Press, 1972), 3.

The essential organs provide fertile nourishment, if in metaphor alone. Haruspicy is a form of divination that involves reading the entrails of sacrificed animals, in some cases to reveal truths about the mysteries of the human body—physical aberration, illness, projected courses of healing. Examine the organs, what remains, and in them see the life of an entire body. Eat of the heart, even your own, and experience the bitter revelations of all that hides within the fleshy joy of human tissue: hold it in the air for all to see, fine beating alchemy. But, *Alas, the heart is not a metaphor—or not only a metaphor.*[67]

The narrating voice of Plath's 'Mystic' asks, *Is there no great love, only tenderness? / Does the sea // Remember the walker upon it?*[68] To remember, always, that any body, that every body, once lived.

This body was angry and scared, jubilant and exhilarated—this body loved and hurt and fell and got up again—this body wrote stories and poems and hoped and felt foolish and was brilliant nonetheless—this body tried hard to hide what was wrong—this body was a child who carried a heavy school bag, it dug into her shoulders—this body missed her father after he died—this body was a baby whose mother nursed and held it—this body was lonely—this body had electrodes placed on her temples and felt every violent shock as though she was being tortured—this body wondered what she was being punished for—this body had her own babies and held and nursed and loved them—this body tried and failed and failed again and failed better—or worse—depending on who you ask.

In 'Laugh of the Medusa', Cixous writes, *If there is a 'propriety of woman', it is paradoxically her capacity to depropriate unselfishly, body without end, without appendage, without principal 'parts'...This doesn't mean that she's undifferentiated magma, but*

67 Elizabeth Hardwick, *Sleepless Nights* (New York: New York Review of Books, 2001), 91.

68 Plath, 'Mystic', in *Collected Poems*, 269.

that she doesn't lord it over her body or her desire…Her libido is cosmic, just as her unconscious is worldwide. Her writing can only keep going, without ever inscribing or discerning contours.[69] At the end of the day, empathy is the tenderest alchemy, so intimately bound with imagination and understanding. Everything in pieces, memories, flashes — scattered linguistic exhalations of the body, mind and heart, with no longing for specious unity.

When Plath read 'Lady Lazarus' in a reading prepared for the BBC, she introduced it by explaining, *The speaker is a woman who has the great and terrible gift of being reborn. The only trouble is, she has to die first. She is the Phoenix, the libertarian spirit, what you will. She is also just a good, plain, very resourceful woman.*[70] The poem is often interpreted as a detailing of Plath's own suicide attempts, three in number, with one final success. But I like the idea of the Phoenix being also just a *good, plain, very resourceful woman* — foremost in her arsenal of resources, a talent not just for dying, but for life-sustaining poetry that cannot expire, that continues to write itself into the future. In one of the Lady's attempts at death she *rocked shut // As a seashell. / They had to call and call / And pick the worms off me like sticky pearls.*[71] A metaphorical nod, perhaps, to Ariel's song in *The Tempest*, which haunts the margins of much of Plath's oeuvre:

Full fathom five thy father lies;
Of his bones are coral made;
Those are pearls that were his eyes:
Nothing of him that doth fade,
But doth suffer a sea-change
Into something rich and strange.

69 Hélène Cixous, 'The Laugh of the Medusa', trans. Keith Cohen and Paula Cohen, *Signs* 1, no. 4 (Summer 1976): 875–93, at 889.

70 Plath, 'Notes: 1962', in *Collected Poems*, 292.

71 Plath, 'Lady Lazarus', in *Collected Poems*, 245.

Plath's maggots glitter and flash, rotting opalescent figments carefully preserved as jewels to be admired at a later date for their potential to reveal, like shimmering pearls, the entirety of distant worlds reached only by a mind turning and turning in its own depths of contemplation — endless fathoms of fathoming.

Something rich and strange.

They had to call and call.

In 'Last Words', Plath outlines a funeral in which the speaker imagines what will happen to her body — what rites and passages, what gains and losses — after she dies: *I do not want a plain box, she says, I want a sarcophagus / With tigery stripes, and a face on it / Round as the moon, to stare up. / I want to be looking at them when they come.*[72] The voice of this poem worries about her spirit escaping like steam, *One day it won't come back,* and imagines that the blue eye of her turquoise will comfort when the soles of her feet grow cold. Surrounded by tokens that purr with warmth and happy scents, she dissolves into the constellation of her afterlife to come — dark and content.

Let me have my copper cooking pots, let my rouge pots
Bloom about me like night flowers, with a good smell.
They will roll me up in bandages, they will store my heart
Under my feet in a neat parcel.
I shall hardly know myself. It will be dark,
And the shine of these small things sweeter than the face of Ishtar.[73]

I hope that of all, of any of the parts that remain, for Plath, or for me or for you — for any body, for every body — this is the case. And I hope we are looking at them when they come and that our last words are our own.

---

72 Plath, 'Last Words', in *Collected Poems*, 172.

73 Ibid.

Acknowledgements

This is a book of bodies and movement and patience. There are an endless number of people I would like to say thank you to, for their continual support, encouragement, their dissolving of worry, and for their patience.

punctum books is where I should start. Thank you for taking on the project when it was only the silhouette of the book it has become. And for keeping ideas open; for creating a publishing house which remains unconventional and radical.

To my family — thank you for your constant brilliance and support. A huge thank you must go to many of my humans not within the book but so much a part of it, particularly to Isabel Greenberg, for your incredible generosity with time and listening and keeping me on track throughout. Diana Poliacarpo, for capturing and echoing the sounds of the body in music and sharing it with me. To Robert Prouse, for your never-ending enthusiasm for the project and for teaching me patience in myself.

But the book extends beyond itself.

These pages are not really for me, but for the writers and artists and minds in this book and their humans to whom I am grateful too. Because it is our humans that embody the stories we share, who absorb them and turn them into texture; who allow bodies to remain.

— E.B.

ACKNOWLEDGMENTS

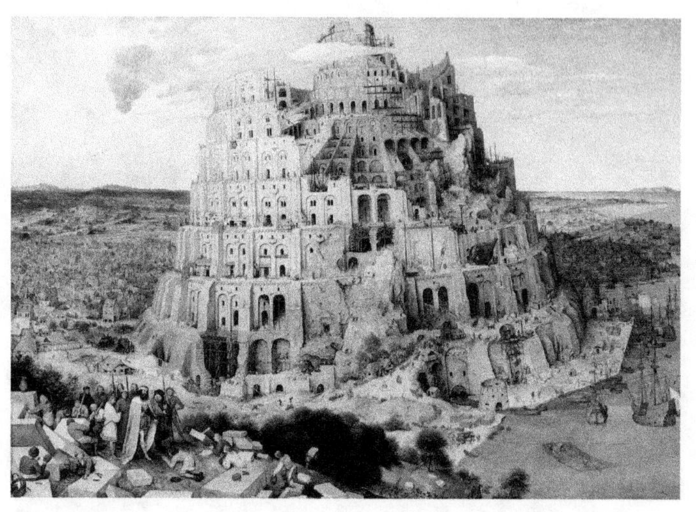

"W. dreams, like Phaedrus, of an army of thinker-friends, thinker-lovers. He dreams of a thought-army, a thought-pack, which would storm the philosophical Houses of Parliament. He dreams of Tartars from the philosophical steppes, of thought-barbarians, thought-outsiders. What distance would shine in their eyes!"

—Lars Iyer

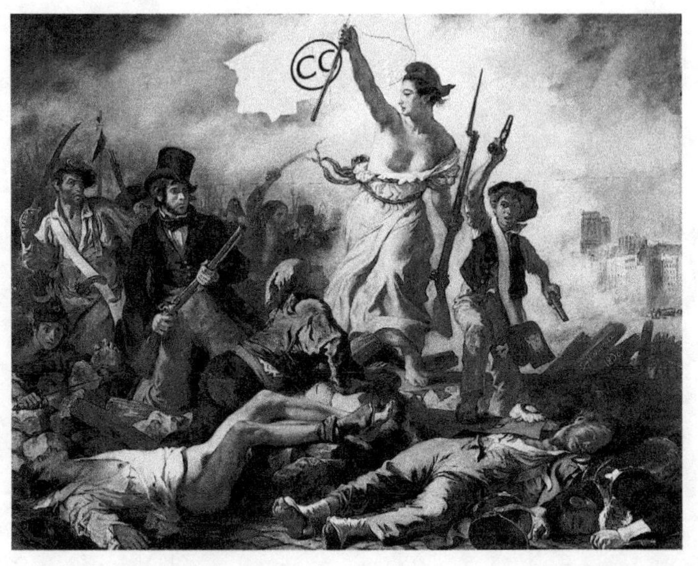
CC

www.ingramcontent.com/pod-product-compliance
Lightning Source LLC
LaVergne TN
LVHW020041110826
845155LV00029B/588

* 9 7 8 1 9 4 7 4 4 7 6 7 7 *